THE BLUEPRINT: STARTING A SUCCESSFUL BUSINESS

A PROVEN 7-PHASE GUIDE TO FIRING YOUR BOSS, GAINING FINANCIAL INDEPENDENCE, AND LIVING THE LIFE OF YOUR DREAMS

KEVIN BARNICLE

Published by Kev Vie Publishing

La Grange, IL, USA

© Copyright KEVIN BARNICLE 2024 - **All rights reserved.**

The content within this book may not be reproduced, duplicated or transmitted without direct written permission from the author or the publisher.

Under no circumstances will any blame or legal responsibility be held against the publisher, or author, for any damages, reparation, or monetary loss due to the information contained within this book. Either directly or indirectly. You are responsible for your own choices, actions, and results.

Legal Notice:

This book is copyright protected. This book is only for personal use. You cannot amend, distribute, sell, use, quote or paraphrase any part, of the content within this book, without the consent of the author or publisher.

Disclaimer Notice:

Please note the information contained within this document is for educational and entertainment purposes only. All effort has been expended to present accurate, up-to-date, and reliable, complete information. No warranties of any kind are declared or implied. Readers acknowledge that the author is not engaging in the rendering of legal, financial, medical or professional advice. The content within this book has been derived from various sources. Please consult a licensed professional before attempting any techniques outlined in this book.

By reading this document, the reader agrees that under no circumstances is the author responsible for any losses, direct or indirect, which are incurred as a result of the use of the information contained within this document, including, but not limited to, — errors, omissions, or inaccuracies.

CONTENTS

Introduction — 5

PHASE ONE
EXPLORATION PHASE
1. Steps to Take in the Months Prior to Firing Your Boss — 11
2. Overcoming Fear and Making the Leap — 23

PHASE TWO
PLANNING AND PRE-LAUNCH
3. Ideation to Innovation—Birthing Your Business Idea — 33
4. Plan Your Work and Work Your Plan—The Business Plan — 41
5. Funding Your Business — 49

PHASE THREE
LAUNCH PHASE—THE BACK END PLUMBING
6. Choosing a Business Name — 63
7. Choosing the Proper Business Structure — 71
8. Legal Requirements and Registrations 101—A Checklist for the New Business — 79
9. Business Finances and Accounting 101 — 89

PHASE FOUR
LAUNCH PHASE—YOU AND MINDSET
10. From Employee to Entrepreneur – The Psychological Blueprint — 99
11. Punching Back—Developing Resilience Practices — 107
12. Understanding the Emotional Toll of the Entrepreneur — 117

PHASE FIVE
BUILDING THE BUSINESS—THE CUSTOMER
13. Building a Customer-Centric Business Model — 133
14. Product Development—Building Winning Products and Solutions — 147
15. Intellectual Property 101 — 153

PHASE SIX
BUILDING THE BUSINESS—THE COMPANY

16. Use the Force—Company Culture as the Heartbeat of the Business ... 161
17. Branding Mastery—Crafting Your Business Identity ... 175
18. Inbound and Out of Bounds—Effective Marketing for the New Business ... 191
19. Building the Sales Team ... 205

PHASE SEVEN
FINANCIAL INDEPENDENCE AND A LIFE WORTH LIVING

20. Exit Strategies and What to Know When Building Your Company ... 219
21. You NEED to Be an Entrepreneur—Maslow's Hierarchy of Needs ... 239
22. The Long-Term Gain ... 247

Reference List ... 257
Appendix ... 261

INTRODUCTION

> *You have brains in your head. You have feet in your shoes. You can steer yourself any direction you choose.*
>
> DR. SEUSS, OH, THE PLACES YOU'LL GO!

I can remember the day and feelings now as clearly as the day it happened. Let me paint the picture for you. I was sitting in an office at work and pacing around the room. I was about to make the biggest decision of my professional life. I was about to fire my boss and leave a high-paying job to start my own business. I was thirty-three years old and had a successful sales career up to that point. But I had zero prior experience starting and running my own company. I was terrified to make the leap but also convinced I should do it. My heart was racing, and my throat was dry as I stood up to walk over to my boss's office. I was dizzy. *Was I making a mistake by quitting? Should I really do this? What the fuck am I doing? It wasn't too late; I could turn back now. Yeah, maybe I should turn back.*

But I didn't. My feet kept moving toward his office as if some unknown force was guiding me. Although I was scared, I was also sick of not feeling in control of my own destiny. I felt like, at any moment, I could be fired. I was fed up with putting my blood, sweat, and tears into my job and management changing it almost annually. I was afraid, but I also told myself I couldn't spend another day working on someone else's dream and wasting another minute sacrificing my own. That day marked the end of my life as an employee and the beginning of my entrepreneurial journey. Since that moment, my life has been more than I ever imagined it could have been, and I wish you the same.

This book is born out of that pivotal moment and the rollercoaster decade ride that followed. Its purpose is simple yet ambitious: to provide you with an easy-to-follow blueprint for starting and building a successful business. Beyond just a guide, this is a collection of my personal experiences, the tools and tactics I used, and a treasure trove of practical information I've picked up along the way.

You might wonder, *Why should I listen to this guy? Who is he to give me advice?* They're fair questions. You should never take advice from someone who hasn't done what you are looking to do. And I wouldn't expect you to either. Trust me, plenty of people who will try to offer you advice in starting a successful business have no business doing so. If you pick up a business book and the author doesn't immediately mention that they have experience actually doing it, run for the hills. As for me, here you go: I started a business with absolutely no prior experience nor a business degree, navigated through a decade of the dizzying maze of entrepreneurship, and emerged on the other side with my company being recognized as one of the top 1,000 fastest-growing companies in the United States. I eventually sold the business for millions of dollars (twice) to a multi-billion-dollar behemoth and retired at forty-five. So yeah, that's why. I've actually walked the path I'm about to guide you on, making me a reliable ally and partner in your entrepreneurial journey.

Then you might ask yourself, *Why is this business book any different or better than all the others?* And I get it. I know there are a ton of business books out there. I have read dozens and dozens myself. You name it, and I have probably read it. Through all of that reading, I know what exists in the marketplace, what type of advice was *actually helpful* when you step into the ring, and what was not covered.

What I wanted to do with *The Blueprint* was create a book I wish I had. One that not only informed me of the steps I needed to take but also shared what worked and what didn't and included insights from the entrepreneur's actual experience. I didn't want to hear from another academic with a PhD or MBA who has never been in the arena (and there are PLENTY of those in the business book world). Those books bored me out of my mind and were essentially no help. I also didn't want some high-level, vanilla two-page summary on essential topics with no lack of detail or practical advice. Yeah, I know how to search the internet, too, pal.

I wanted the raw and the real, not some fluff piece. I didn't want to have to read one hundred books to get the information I needed. I didn't need just a guide; I needed a blueprint. And I didn't want just any blueprint; I wanted THE BLUEPRINT.

That is what sets this guide apart from all the other business books. It's a combination of all I wanted: the step-by-step in great detail, written by a doer, not some academic hiding behind degrees and certifications and sitting behind their desk while the rest of us get our hands dirty in the streets. I mean, really, who cares what they have to say? As an added bonus (#winning), you will get the full Kevvie (what my mom used to call me) experience sprinkled throughout the book, chock-full of expletives, rambling tirades, and my own special form of humor. It's all a part of my "charm," or at least that's what others say. Ok, they don't really say that—I just made that up. I'm sorry. Either way, buckle up, buttercup; shit's about to get real! See, we are making fast friends already.

The book unfolds in seven proven phases, each covering a critical aspect of starting and running a successful business. From the spark of an idea and validating its potential, through the maze of planning out the business and putting the systems in place for success, to strategies for growth and scaling your venture, to ultimately selling and exiting the company (if that is your goal). My journey is peppered throughout each part, offering my personal stories and lessons I learned the hard way.

And I promise that every strategy, tool, and piece of advice has been tested in the real-world arena of business by yours truly. I have the scars to prove it. You'll hear all about the stumbles and triumphs, the doubts and confidence, and the anguish and thrills, reflecting the full spectrum of the rollercoaster entrepreneurial experience.

To you, the aspiring entrepreneur, I understand the mixed bag of excitement, fear, and uncertainty that comes with starting your own business. You're not alone. This book is your ally, mentor, and cheerleader, understanding your aspirations and guiding you through the uncertainties of starting something new.

My hope with this book is that it will be the nudge you need. Yes, entrepreneurship can provide a path to financial independence, but more importantly, it's a journey toward a life filled with purpose and passion. Embrace this adventure, knowing you now have the blueprint to help you navigate the complexities of starting and building a successful business.

Let's face it: life is too short to be living out someone else's dream. It's time to take control of your career and, more importantly, your life. I promise you that when you do, it's incredible how much the world will open itself to you and how much you will learn about yourself in the process. Let's turn your dream into reality together. So, are you ready? Buckle up for the ride of your life. Let's fucking go!

PHASE ONE
EXPLORATION PHASE

This book is broken down into seven essential phases for starting, building, and eventually selling your business (if that is your goal). This first phase explores where you probably are right now: thinking about starting a business but not really sure where to start. In the Exploration Phase, we will talk about practical steps you can take now so you can further educate yourself to help you determine if starting a business is right for you or not, all tested and proven by yours truly. Additionally, we will discuss THE major stumbling block for most wannabe entrepreneurs: fear and how to combat it.

CHAPTER 1
STEPS TO TAKE IN THE MONTHS PRIOR TO FIRING YOUR BOSS

 Fear is a reaction. Courage is a decision.

WINSTON CHURCHILL

Entrepreneurship means many different things to many different people. For most, the "glamour" attributes immediately come to mind: the money, the fame, the power, or the prospects of financial independence. However, one attribute that is not discussed as often, and, I would argue, is even more impressive, is confronting the "scaries" right in the face. But you might be asking yourself: *Dear Kevvie, what exactly are the 'scaries'? Whatchu talking about Willis?* Well, thankfully, you have me to educate you, young Jedi. The scaries are those shadows that lurk in the dark alleys of your mind. And come on, you already know them. They are risk, uncertainty, and the biggest of them all: the fear of failure. Oh, the horror!

This fear can either paralyze you, coaxing you back into the safety net of the status quo, or, alternatively, you can use it as fuel to propel you to a journey marked by growth, resilience, and eventual triumph. Like Neo, it's up to you to take the red pill or the blue pill. Ultimately, your dreams will not reside in the absence of fear but in the mastery of it.

This is the most important step entrepreneurs must overcome: the fear of stepping off the ledge and actually starting the business. That is precisely why I am starting the book off with it. And I get it; I was in the same boat. When I started to have an inkling to start my own company, I had all sorts of inner dialogue pop up, and most of it was unwanted. Think of any of these yet? If not, don't worry, you will. All these thoughts ran through my head:

- What if it's a big failure?
- What will people say about me if it fails?
- What will my wife think about me if it fails?
- Will people make fun of me?
- How can I even think about starting my own business? I don't have any prior experience!
- How can I even think about starting my own business? I don't have a business degree!

All of this is nonsense. If you are hardworking, persistent, and have some level of talent, you will be successful. It's not that complicated.

In early 2011, I was so fed up with my job that I began considering starting a business, but I wasn't sure where to start. For the next nine months until I left my job, I did the following steps, all of which ultimately led to me gaining the courage to make the leap and, in turn, changed my life forever. I am advising you to do the same. These steps will help demystify starting your own business and give you the confidence to overcome your fear and make the leap to control your life.

STEP 1: READ

I do more reading and thinking and make less impulse decisions than most people in business.

WARREN BUFFETT, CEO OF BERKSHIRE HATHAWAY AND ONE OF THE TOP 10 WEALTHIEST PEOPLE ON THE PLANET

I am, by nature, an introvert. When I tell people this, most are flabbergasted and hit me back with a *"UGH, NO, YOU ARE NOT!"* Because, ya know, I am not quiet and, as you have already witnessed, can be obnoxious. But it's true. Usually, when I have something on my mind, I just don't ramble about it to anyone. I have to sit and think before I get to that stage.

Therefore, what I usually do when something tickles my fancy is seek out information. My favorite source of information is books. I read a lot—somewhere in the neighborhood of fifty to one hundred books a year (aided by teaching myself how to speed-read). And maybe you are the same. Hell, you picked up this book, right? So not only are you most likely the same in your love of reading, but by God, you also have impeccable taste. And you are already taking my advice! You beautiful son of a bitch, you. See? We really are making fast friends.

And you are now doing precisely what I did, which is to read and become more educated on the topic. I read a ton of the different business books that were available at the time. The books were all over the map. Some were more prescriptive on specific technical aspects of starting a business, like securing funding or the difference between legal structures; some focused more on the customer-focused elements of a business, such as sales or marketing, and others on selling a company. But what I found the most helpful were books that were written in more plain speech by authors who had actually started a business from scratch and recounted how they did it.

The two books that stood out to me the most at the time (this was in 2011) as being helpful were *The Toilet Paper Entrepreneur* by Mike Michalowicz and *The Four-Hour Work Week* by the brilliant Tim Ferriss. These books inspired me early in my process and really got my gears going. Both gave practical advice, and I could tell both writers had "been there and done that." In this book, I will talk about some of the lessons I learned from these two specific books (as well as others) and how they helped me overcome the fears of starting the company.

Once I read about ten books, I had a good sense of what was involved and felt more educated. That made me more confident and excited to move on to the next step, digging into not only if I should do it but how I could do it. My hope is that you will only need to read this particular book to get to that same step, and I have designed it with that thought in mind. If it doesn't (it's ok; we can still be friends), I have provided a complete index of book suggestions and will highlight many of the lessons from those books throughout here.

But anyway, congratulations, as you are already having success. By reading this book, you passed the first step in the process, and you didn't even know it! You overachiever, you! See, you got this shit. On to the next.

STEP 2: FIND AND TALK TO PEOPLE WHO HAVE STARTED THEIR OWN BUSINESS

The fastest way to change yourself is to hang out with people who are already the way you want to be.

REID HOFFMAN, CO-FOUNDER OF LINKEDIN

When I was considering starting a company, only a handful of people I knew had actually done it (you too soon will join this rarified air). I truly believe that entrepreneurs are the chosen ones—they propel the world forward. In the immortal words of the brilliant Steve Jobs, "The ones who are crazy enough to think they can change the world are the ones that do." But having said all of that, entrepreneurs are also rare, as most people would rather live a "safe" life controlled by others.

So I reached out to each one I knew, told them what I was doing, and asked if I could take them out to lunch and bend their ear. I promise you that they will eventually take your meeting. Successful entrepreneurs love sharing their stories and encouraging others to do as they did, as the entrepreneurial life is an uncommon approach but a life well-lived.

The first person I reached out to was my buddy Marc Lifshin, someone I used to work with who had started a real estate development company. As I wanted to start a technology services company, his business had zero in common with mine. But it didn't matter, and it won't matter to you. Just find anyone you can who has started their own company. You just want to make starting your own business a realistic option and demystify—and frankly de-glorify—the process for you.

My meeting with Marc was great. I explained what I was thinking and asked him about his entrepreneurial experience. I heard about all the ups and downs of running your own business (yes, there are downs to running your own company, but there are plenty of downs in having a "stable" job). It was so inspiring and grounding to talk to someone who did it. I remember thinking, "This is just a normal guy. There is nothing spectacular about him. Yes, he's smart and a good dude, but if he can do it, I can too." And that is precisely what he told me as well. I came out of that meeting incredibly energized.

Fast forward to today. I have had lunches or meetings with dozens, if not hundreds, of business owners. I can tell you that not one, NOT A SINGLE ONE, ever regretted it, including him. That doesn't mean they were all smashing successes—there indeed were failures, but none regretted doing it. What does that say to you about this potential adventure? For me, it says a ton. Think about that: not a single person. Marc's company, Core Spaces, is now one of the leading real estate investment managers, developers and operators specializing in student housing in the country, and we started together as a couple of knucklehead copier salespeople. If he and I can do it, you can do it too.

The next guy I met with had a company I wouldn't compete with but was in the same industry, so I felt it would be particularly helpful. We went out to lunch, and I asked him a bunch of questions. I didn't know this guy as well personally, but I had done business with his company in the past. The lunch was all over the place. He was scatterbrained, kept looking at his phone, and told me about some drama he had with his business partner. He was a good dude and everything, but I remember thinking, "Man, if this guy can do this, I can DEFINITELY do this." Once again, it demystified starting a business for me, even though it was for different reasons than the first meeting.

After meeting with these two, there was one guy I really wanted to meet with but didn't know personally. His name was Dan Adamany. Although I didn't know him, I knew about him as he was in my industry and worked at the same company I was at previously. Additionally, he basically did exactly what I was going to do: start a tech services company and reseller, albeit against different technologies than I was focusing on. I reached out to a friend of mine, Matt McElwee, who I used to work with but who was now at Dan's company. I told him I was thinking about quitting and starting a business and asked if I could ask him about working for a tech reseller. Matt and I had lunch, and after I shared what I was planning on, Matt said, "You have to talk to Dan."

I remember being excited that Matt was willing to make the introduction. Still, I was also sober at the likelihood of it happening. Dan was super successful and busy, and I figured he wouldn't have time to meet with me. Matt asked Dan, and to my surprise, Dan did agree to meet with me. In our first meeting, Dan and I hit it off, and over the next nine months, while I contemplated starting the business, he graciously met with me four times so I could ask him further questions. Many of the lessons I will discuss in this book, especially about overcoming the fear, come from those meetings.

In my first meeting with Dan, I wanted to ensure I used his time as efficiently as possible. I walked in, introduced myself, and said, "Hey, I am not sure if Matt told you, but I am thinking about starting a business. But I have zero experience and have no clue what I am doing. If you are good with it, I would just like to lay out everything to you, and you tell me if I am an idiot or not." He smiled and said sure thing.

I just took him through everything for about ten minutes, and he asked questions throughout. When I finished spewing, he looked at me and said, "You need to quit your job today and start this company TOMORROW!" I was floored. *Exsqueeze me? What did he just say?* That was NOT what I was expecting.

Being the eloquent communicator that I am, I hit him back with a *"Huh?"* Like a teenage boy going through puberty, my voice cracked, and I continued, "Um… I am not sure I am ready to quit tomorrow, man; I am still planning it out." He challenged me again, "What do you mean? Opportunities like this don't always present themselves. You have to get going right away!" I continued about how I had two little kids and a wife who didn't work. He understood but continued with me, "What are you so scared of?"

I rattled off a few reasons, mainly because I didn't feel prepared yet. Ok, that at least he could understand. So, Dan sent me home with an exercise: write a business plan, which would help me think through everything. When I told him I had never done one, he said, "Don't worry about it. Just do a rough and tough one. It doesn't have to be perfect. It's all about the exercise." Additionally, he said, "But write it as if you are going to show it to and pitch investors on the idea, even if you have zero plans to. Because if the audience is not just you, it will help you think through it more. Either way, at the end of the process, you will be either more or less confident about doing it, and that is the point."

STEP 3: WRITE A ROUGH DRAFT BUSINESS PLAN

So I did. And you should, too. This was the first time I had written a business plan. *Shit, where do I even start?* I went with the old-fashioned tried and true plan of googling one, pulling up a template, and just getting after it. For shits and giggles, I am including the exact one I did. Here it is: https://bit.ly/BlueprintRoughDraftBusinessPlan

Later in the book, I will discuss the specifics of writing a detailed business plan, but before you get into the more "polished" version, I want you to write a down-and-dirty one. Mine will look comically stupid and not polished. And that's fine—looking back at it now, I laugh (and cringe). The point of this exercise is to get your thoughts down on paper so you can think more clearly and reduce the thoughts of failure that will ultimately come. As you review mine, most of the details won't make sense to you, so just ignore those and focus on the high-level structure. Mine was just thoughts dumped on paper, and that's precisely the point.

You don't need to spend much more than an hour on this; the purpose is to get all those ideas rolling around your head out on paper. You can refine it later. Regardless of whether you use mine or a different template, here are the basics you want to include:

Executive Summary: For this, you want to write down what you are trying to do at a high level. As you can see in mine, I detailed our objectives, mission, and major keys to success.

Company Summary: This is the "who" slide. Discuss who will be in the business on day one and who you foresee potentially joining in the first 12 months. You will want to detail any office locations, including a home office.

Products and services: Write down what products and services you are considering selling on day one and discuss any known competitors' products and services. You can also write down any other products or services you are considering but won't be available initially.

Market analysis: Detail out who you will be targeting as customers. Talk about the market segment you will go after and what general needs you will fill in the marketplace. Further, write down any current market trends, the size of the market and anticipated growth rates, and any known buying patterns.

Strategy summary: Talk about your initial sales, pricing, and marketing strategies.

Management summary: Write down the management team and any known personnel gaps that you know you need to fill. You don't need to have all the answers right now; it's just about identifying what you need to figure out afterward.

Financial plan: talk about how you will fund the company and, if you have any hard fixed costs like salaries on day one, how you will break even every month.

That's it! Once again, this is not supposed to be polished. You just want to get everything rattling around that noggin out and onto paper. Once you do this, you can objectively examine it and consider what you would need to do to fill in any gaps.

Ok, so now that you have done the three exercises (reading, meeting people, and writing the business plan), you are probably feeling much more confident and prepared. You are going to take on the world! But before we get ahead of ourselves, we have to pause and look at our personal finances and determine how much runway we have.

STEP 4: DO A BUDGETING EXERCISE ON YOUR PERSONAL NEEDS

I will get into budgeting for your business and funding strategies later in the book, but this is more about your and your family's (if applicable) personal finance needs. This is about determining how much money you have and how long it will last before you have to look at alternative options or pull the rip cord.

Now, some people have a great understanding of how much money they need and or spend every month, and some have no clue. I was in the middle. As I was in sales, I was never on a set income. I had a base salary, but in a typical year, more than fifty percent of my income was variable based on commissions, i.e., the income I received for selling whatever I was selling. I always lived below my means, so I rarely stressed about money. Because I had a decent but not-great understanding of everything my wife and I were spending, I decided to do a deeper dive analysis. Many tools are out there, many of them free, that you can use to do this. The one that I used was Mint that you can find at www.mint.com. It's essentially an application that connects to your bank accounts and credit cards and creates a dashboard to see all your money coming in and going out. It can be eye-opening when you see some of your trends played out in front of you (Jesus, how much are we spending on ice cream for the kids? Screw you, Cold Stone). It can categorize some charges automatically, like gas or groceries, but you can also tag your other expenses and set up rules for going forward. The whole process only took me a few hours.

When that is complete, you can get a REAL look at your spending. Here is a high-level summary of what mine looked like.

- Primary residence mortgage payment, including taxes and insurance: $3,800 per month
- Car payment (one car was paid off): $380 per month
- Private school for two kids: $700 per month
- Groceries: $500 per month
- Entertainment: $400 per month
- Vacation budget for the year: $250 per month

All in all, it was around $7,500 per month, which was the exact number I used as the budget. I had $75,000 in personal savings that I could use for my own individual needs and $75,000 that I was going to put into the company. I planned on not taking a salary in the first year. I wasn't sure if I would be able to, but for this exercise, let's assume you will not. It doesn't mean your business won't be profitable (mine made plenty of profit), but most likely, if things are going well, you will reinvest those profits in the company to grow.

Looking at my finances, I now knew I had ten months to survive without a single dollar coming into my personal account. The idea of that is scary, yes. In one of my early meetings with Dan, he told me that I would know if the business would be successful or not after six months and that if it wasn't working, I could always get another job. So, after looking at it through the six-month lens, it actually wasn't that scary. I told myself, *Ok, as Dan said, I will know if the company will be successful after six months. If it isn't, I will look for another job. And that gives me four months before I run out of money to find a job.* So, although it was scary, I also looked at it objectively, and as long as I stuck to my six-month rule, I was good.

I highly recommend you go through this exercise and get a good gauge for yourself. Once you break down these thoughts, things become way less scary. It doesn't mean the fear won't go away; it won't. Plan on that. But you will be better prepared to handle the fear.

Now you might be saying to yourself, *Well shit, Kevin, I don't have $75,000.* That is totally fine. The dollar amount is less significant than how many months of the runway you have. I personally felt comfortable with my ten-month window on the six-month rule. You may be more of a risk-taker. Maybe you are more conservative. Either way, knowing and understanding yourself is fundamental. You can argue that it's the most important trait an entrepreneur can have. You will have to look at your own situation and expense ratios. But it will help you make an informed decision.

After going through these steps, things will become much clearer. Either you will feel invigorated or maybe less confident. Either way, that's a positive step in determining whether you want to start the company.

These are the exact steps that I did, and I can tell you my experience is that after I went through these steps, I was chomping at the fucking bit to get going. As Ayn Rand said, "The question isn't who is going to let me; it's who is going to stop me." When you start thinking about the art of what is possible and owning your own business, which has unlimited possibilities, you WILL feel alive. And what better feeling to have as a human? For me, this process woke something up in me that I never knew even existed. I could not stop thinking about doing it. I had dreams about it almost every night. After going through these exercises, I was very confident my business would succeed, and I loved how I felt. I felt ALIVE. I told myself that fuck it, I was going to do it. Now, I had to look at the next steps to take to make the actual leap. Let's do the same for you.

CHAPTER 2
OVERCOMING FEAR AND MAKING THE LEAP

> *All our dreams can come true, if we have the courage to pursue them.*
>
> WALT DISNEY, CO-FOUNDER OF THE WALT DISNEY COMPANY

Ok, I had done it. I had gone through the exercises to make this dream a reality. I had read books and became informed about starting a business. I talked to real-life people who had done what I wanted to do. I had done my rough and tough business plan. And I had figured out how much money I personally needed to survive. I felt great! I was ready to take on the world. Now, I just had to figure out my exit strategy from my existing company. And this is where the anxiety really kicks in.

As you approach getting closer and closer to the day you will leave your job and step into the unknown, the fears and anxieties of starting your own business will intensify. Count on it. But this is normal. In my last meeting with Dan, before I made the leap, I told him I was feeling very anxious. He told me he understood, but then again, as all good mentors do, he challenged me. Dan knew I had children. He said to me, "Imagine your son or daughter came to you in twenty years and explained this very opportunity to you. What would your advice be to them?" I smiled and said, "Go for it." He replied, "Exactly." This conversation, as well as an exercise I did, wound up helping me eventually overcome the fears.

Before we get into the exercise, let's talk a little bit about fear itself. What exactly is fear? Fear is simply an emotional response to a perceived threat or danger. It is a fundamental survival mechanism that triggers a range of physiological and psychological reactions. Regarding starting a business, the fear of failure gets heightened the most. The first step toward overcoming this fear of failure is pinpointing its roots. Often, these fears stem from a blend of personal and societal pressures: the dread of losing financial stability, the apprehension of tarnishing one's reputation, or the simple, gut-wrenching thought of not being good enough. Recognizing these fears requires honest self-reflection.

So, how do you reflect on it? During my read phase in the nine months before firing my boss, I was introduced to a "fear-setting" exercise detailed in *The Four-Hour Work Week*.

In fear-setting, you write down your biggest fears about a particular subject. Then, you distill them further into worse-case, dooms-day, sky-falls-apart scenarios. The idea is to clarify the nature of these fears and categorize them into what is even remotely realistic, what can be controlled, and what cannot. Once you do, you can recognize how ridiculous most of your fears are. So, my personal exercise looked like this. I tried to think of the absolute worst things that could happen. Here were all the fears I had (in order of how they could go down):

- Company fails
- Public embarrassment
- Losing money
- Feeling shame
- Wife leaves me
- I lose my house
- I can never find another job
- I wind up homeless, and my family won't talk to me

The idea is to basically show you how ridiculous your fears really are. As I started thinking about all these things, what was REALLY the realistic outcome of what would happen if I failed? Let's look at mine one by one.

FEAR 1: THE COMPANY FAILING

Ok, let's say the company did fail. This one, when you look at the statistics, is plausible. It's ridiculous how many sources you will hear about the failure rate of new businesses. Still, a general one you will commonly hear is that about fifty percent of new businesses fail in the first five years. Ok, fine, we will go with that for this exercise. So, half of companies fail, but that also means half *succeed*. For me, the upside of owning my own company was MASSIVE. I could take control of my future. Financial independence was a real possibility. I could capitalize on my hard work and not let someone take that from me. I would have freedom. There were potential untold financial windfalls. I could set myself and my family up for life. So yeah, the upside significantly outweighed the downside. Sure, there are some downsides if the company fails, which I will detail below, but I also felt very confident and knew myself well. I knew that I would be ALL IN and that I would work my ass off until it succeeded. If you subscribe to the same "failure is not an option" ethos as I do, this fear will be eliminated, as it was for me. On to the next.

FEAR 2: PUBLIC EMBARRASSMENT

One of the other things that popped into my head about what would happen if the company failed was I would feel some public embarrassment. In general, I identify myself as a winner as I typically have success in whatever I put my mind to. So, what would people think of me if it failed? Oh, the horror! But at the end of the day, I thought to myself, *Who really gives a shit?* The older I get, the more and more I realize that people are NOT thinking about you; they are thinking about themselves. So would anyone besides my immediate family really give a shit? Nope. As the old saying goes, "Those that matter don't mind, and those that mind don't matter." Amen. Cross this one off the list and move on to the next.

FEAR 3: LOSING MONEY

On to the next one, losing money. Ok, yeah, fine. This one was realistic if things didn't go well. I had $75,000 from a 401k that I used to fund the company (more on this later). In one of my meetings with Dan, we discussed the possibility of losing this money. He said, "Fine, maybe the company will fail, and you will lose that 75k. But you are young, and you will make it back. Also, you can't touch that money until you are sixty anyway. Think about how much it will turn into IF THINGS GO RIGHT." So yeah, 75k was literally my retirement savings, but I was thirty-three and couldn't touch it until I was sixty. And what's a better investment: investing money into something I can't control or influence, like a stock market index, or investing that money into myself, something I can completely control and believe in? Once again, the reward greatly outweighed the risk. Checked off and move on.

FEAR 4: FEELING SHAME

Up next, we have "feeling shame." As I got close to making the leap, I admitted to Dan that I was feeling apprehensive about it. He asked me specifically what my fears were, and I was honest and told him this was one. He challenged me with, "Feeling shame about whose opinions? Other people? People who never did what you did? Why in the world would you care about anyone's opinions who didn't have the courage you had?" He expanded, "Anyone who started their own company, whether it was successful or not, would understand and be proud you had the courage to do it. So they certainly wouldn't feel shame toward you."

The next one hit me right square in the jaw. He continued, "You should only care about your feelings. I PROMISE YOU, if the company fails, you will feel zero shame about yourself if you give it your all. You will be one of the very few who decided to have the courage to chase your dreams. What's more heroic than that?" It really struck a chord with me. And, per usual, he was right. The day I walked out of the office and fired my boss, I was incredibly proud of myself. I was proud that I had the courage despite the unclear outcome. That pride in yourself gives you incredible strength in the early days. As I look back now, even though my ride wound up being successful, I am so goddamn proud of myself for that day. I wish I could go back, give myself a hug, and say, "It's going to work out." I am hoping this book will serve as that hug you need. So yeah, shame, especially personal shame, was crossed the fuck off.

FEAR 5: MY WIFE LEAVING ME

The next step I had to overcome was the fear of my wife leaving me if things did not go well with the company. The more I thought about it, the more I realized it was a ridiculous notion. My wife was incredibly encouraging and on board with my idea of starting the company. A week before I quit my job, I received a promotion offer that I had seriously considered. I told my wife about it, and she acted disinterestedly. I asked her, "Why aren't you more excited about this?" and she replied, "Because starting your own business is YOUR DREAM." Does that sound like someone who would leave me if things didn't go right? I am not saying every spouse would be this supportive, but mine certainly was. So, look at your own situation, but for me, this fear was stuffed in the "ridiculous" category. So once again, I couldn't control that the thought popped into my head, but it did. So, just dissecting it became incredibly valuable.

FEAR 6: LOSING MY HOUSE

On to the next fear: losing my house. I was proud of the fact that my sales career allowed my wife and I to buy a house, and it was a beautiful house. I decided going in that I absolutely refused, no matter what, to put my family in that position and even openly talked about it with my wife. I said to her, "Look, I am not going to touch a single cent of the home equity in the house, and if after six months the company isn't doing well and we are running out of money, I will go get another job so we won't lose the house." I knew I was disciplined enough to live by this rule, and I did. Even years later, when my company needed cash desperately because a customer was not paying a large bill, I refused to touch my home equity. There was no way I was going to lose the house. So, this one was also checked off.

FEAR 7: NEVER FINDING ANOTHER JOB

And onto my last fear, I had come up with never finding another job. In one of my conversations with Dan, I discussed this with him. He laughed and said, "Haven't you been your company's number-one sales guy for years? Do you not think they would take you back in a heartbeat? Or their competition wouldn't hire you in a second? Shit, I will hire you. I will tell you right now that you have a job here if things don't work out. But you won't need it. Even if it does fail and people see it on your resume, they will give you credit because you had the courage to do it, and that shows confidence in your own ability. And that is a desirable trait." He was right on all of it. I even started laughing at how absurd the thought was.

So, as you can see, as long as you can objectively look at your fears, you will see they are never as scary as they appear on the surface. Your action item is to do a fear-setting exercise. Right now, write down your biggest fears, even ones that sound ridiculous, and put them on paper. Then, break them down. Are they really that realistic? And if so (some of them will have some merit), write down what you can do to mitigate or lessen it. I promise this will make you feel better. It won't necessarily reduce the fears completely, but it gives you a roadmap of what to do IF things go wrong. And once again, you will know if your business will be successful after six months, so look at it through that lens.

I can't stress how important this step is. I have talked to dozens of aspiring entrepreneurs about starting their own company. They always want to know what my "secret sauce" was to start my own company with no experience, sell it twice, and retire at forty-five. The whole thing seems preposterous to them. They must all come in thinking I am some savant or something (trust me, I am not; I am as average as anyone else out there). Want to know what my response is to their question? It is always just a simple one-word response, "Courage."

Truly, this is the case. The rest of starting and running a business is not rocket science. It's figuring it out along the way and surrounding yourself with a good team. I firmly believe that if they are persistent and hard working, 90% of the people in the world would be successful starting their own business if they just had the COURAGE to do it. But this IS the major stumbling block: never getting out of the gates.

Most people will tell themselves they are not good enough, don't have enough experience, or whatever other neurosis they have. It's all bullshit. You ARE good enough, and experience is overrated. If you have grit, work hard, and really care about what you are doing, you will succeed. And the upside FAR exceeds the downside. So, stop thinking about what could go wrong and start thinking about what could go right.

Got it? Get it? Good. Now that you have faced your fears, dared to believe in yourself, and taken control of the reins of your life, we will now move on to the next step of giving birth to your business.

PHASE TWO
PLANNING AND PRE-LAUNCH

In the Planning and Pre-launch phase, we will discuss the activities we must do before launching the business, how to come up with and test your business idea, and how to develop a thorough business plan. Finally, we will discuss funding the company and the different options available to you.

CHAPTER 3
IDEATION TO INNOVATION—BIRTHING YOUR BUSINESS IDEA

> *Business opportunities are like buses, there's always another one coming.*
>
> RICHARD BRANSON, FOUNDER OF VIRGIN GROUP

The spark of a business idea often ignites in the quiet moments; perhaps it's during a run when your mind wanders or during a conversation with a friend about life's challenges. Or it can be in moments of frustration where you are determined to find a better way. These flickers of inspiration, which can be seemingly insignificant at the time, hold the potential to transform into the blazing fire of a successful business. Because inspiration surrounds us, the real challenge lies in massaging these raw ideas into viable business concepts that stand the test of market demands and personal passion.

Consider Uber's origins. Let's hear from Travis Kalanick, Uber's Founder: "Uber came out of a snowy evening in Paris when my friend and I couldn't get a cab. We realized there's a big problem with the current taxi system and thought we could solve it with technology."

Or Kevin Systrom of Instagram: "I was on a vacation in Mexico and was lamenting how my photos didn't look as good as professional's. I thought about making an app that could make it easy for anyone to share beautiful photos in a simple way."

Or Sara Blakely of Spanx: "I was getting ready for a party and realized I didn't have the right undergarment that would not show under white pants. Frustrated by the options available, I took scissors and cut the feet off my pantyhose. It was the a-ha moment that started it all."

For me, the type of business I wanted to start was more of a slow burn but became very obvious, so obvious that I decided I HAD to do it. I was at a large Fortune 500 company, EMC Corporation, selling a software solution to attorneys to help them find electronic documents due to a lawsuit or investigation. The challenge was that after I sold it to them, they wouldn't use it for a few months until the next lawsuit or investigation hit, and then they wouldn't remember how to use it. They needed a team to run the tool for them, but their internal IT teams were busy with other responsibilities, and most attorneys were not technically savvy enough to do it themselves.

I surveyed the market and tried to find an outside company to help. Even though there were a few, they were either a) doing a lousy job or b) not committed to the platform these customers owned. This kept happening over and over, and finally, I told my company, "There is a business here; customers need people to run these tools, and no one is helping them." The company I was at, EMC Corporation, was not a services company; they were a hardware and software company. They informed me they weren't interested in creating the business, so I decided I would. I was in a meeting and told an executive at the company, "Well, if you don't do it, I am going to do it." It just popped out of my mouth. To my surprise, he didn't completely shut me down and even talked to me about the reality of doing it, as he had considered it in the past as well. To me, there was a very clear market demand, and it felt like I had identified a no-brainer opportunity. Many successful businesses launched similarly, simply responding to clear market demands. The key is to keep your eyes and ears open.

But just because that is the route I took doesn't mean it is the right route for you. Obviously, there are a million different businesses out there that you can create. Hopefully, you have some sense of what you want to do already, but if not, here is a guideline to help you determine one.

INTERSECTING PASSION WITH MARKET NEEDS

One of the critical principles to look at when starting a business is identifying something that has a personal interest to you and that you are passionate about. The combo of personal interest and market need marks the sweet spot for successful business ideas. This was true for me. As I was the son of an attorney and had grown up working in a law firm, I found law and lawyers interesting. Beyond finding law interesting, I have always been interested in computers and technology, even as a little kid. So, I particularly found the confluence of technology and law intriguing and something I was interested in pursuing as a career.

Further, being raised by an attorney and interacting with attorneys all my life, I understood them and was comfortable working with them. I can tell you that even today, many people are VERY UNCOMFORTABLE working with attorneys. So, combining my love of technology and strong understanding of attorneys was not only an area that I found fascinating but one that I felt uniquely qualified to succeed at. When you are thinking about what type of business to create, always look through the lens of something you are passionate about and/or something you are uniquely qualified to address.

If you are still unsure what type of business to create, let's examine some idea-generation techniques.

IDEA-GENERATION TECHNIQUES

You can take several different approaches to come up with business ideas. Here are some widely used techniques:

1. Consume/Produce Approach: The "consume-produce" approach to business idea generation involves examining the products and services you regularly use (consume) and identifying gaps, inefficiencies, or opportunities for improvement that you could address by creating (producing) a new business or product. If you are consuming a lot of something, you probably have a good sense of what is good and what is not and how to improve things.

This is the approach I used to produce this book. I am retired but young, and I still want to do activities that interest me but bring in passive income. I looked at what I consumed a lot of. As mentioned earlier, I have read dozens and dozens of business books, so in other words, I have consumed many of them. I know what books worked for me, which ones didn't, and what was missing in the field. So, I decided to produce my own business book. If you want wealth, you have to produce, not consume. So look at what you consume a lot of and think about how you could produce something different or better.

2. Brainstorming: This is one of the most straightforward and commonly used methods. It involves gathering a group of people, discussing a specific idea or challenge, and freely sharing thoughts and ideas without judgment about a particular topic or challenge. The key is to generate many ideas and get them down on paper to be refined and evaluated later. This is the old "Throw shit against the wall and see what sticks" approach.

3. Pain and Gain Analysis: This involves identifying customer pain points (problems customers are experiencing) and gaining creators (how a product or service can provide benefits). By analyzing these aspects, new products or services that address these pains and gains can be devised.

I was asked to present to a local high school's Entrepreneur Club a few years back. I told them that when thinking of a business, it can be broken down simply by a company doing one of two things: helping people decrease pain or helping them increase pleasure. You can categorize every business into one of these categories. Want an example? I hate cutting the lawn. My dad always made me do it as a kid, and I hated it. It was always scorching hot outside; wet grass and bugs would get all over me, it would take seemingly forever, and I constantly had to stop to pick up dog shit. As a result, I avoid cutting the grass like a plague as an adult. It gives me pain to think about cutting grass, so I outsource it to a company that does it for me. Otherwise, I love going on vacations and traveling, which gives me great pleasure. I love the feeling of going somewhere new and foreign to me. I feel alive. And I am not alone. That is why travel and entertainment are multi-billion-dollar industries.

You are either helping people decrease pain or increase pleasure. Think through things that cause you a lot of pain that you could help solve or what items or experiences you love and could enhance. People likely have the same pains and loves.

4. Blue Ocean Strategy: This strategy, named after the book of the same title, involves finding or creating a new market space (the "Blue Ocean") where there is no competition instead of competing in overcrowded industries (the "Red Ocean"). This can lead to highly innovative business ideas that open new markets. As Peter Thiel once said, "Competition is for losers. If you want to create and capture lasting value, look to build a monopoly." Blue Ocean strategies can lead to highly innovative business ideas that open brand-new markets.

5. The Five Whys: Originally part of lean manufacturing, this technique involves asking "Why?" repeatedly, just like my teenagers do, or precisely five times, to get to the root of a problem. Once the fundamental issue is identified, new solutions can be developed, leading to innovative business ideas.

6. Trend Analysis: Monitoring market and industry trends can provide insights into future demands. This method involves analyzing these trends to create products or services that align with the market's direction. We will discuss tools and strategies for market and trend analysis later in the book. As of this writing, in 2024, artificial intelligence (AI) is really taking off and is a massive market trend. As a result, I get emails about investing in the multitude of AI startups every week. They are simply chasing the market trends, and you see this play out over and over again.

SCAMPER: This technique encourages new ways of thinking about existing products or services. SCAMPER stands for Substitute, Combine, Adapt, Modify, Put to another use, Eliminate, and Reverse. By asking questions based on these verbs, one can create new ideas based on old ones.

Each of these methodologies offers different perspectives and can be used in various combinations to generate compelling and innovative business ideas. My advice would be to start with a single approach and, if it doesn't work, move on to the next technique.

ASSESSING YOUR IDEA'S POTENTIAL

Once you identify your business idea, it's necessary to evaluate the viability of it. Here are the markers to look at:

- **Market Demand**: Is there a clear, unmet need for your product or service?
- **Passion Alignment**: Does this idea ignite your enthusiasm and leverage your strengths?
- **Differentiation**: How does your idea stand out from existing offerings?
- **Scalability**: Can this business grow in size, market reach, and revenue?
- **Monetization**: How am I going to make money on this idea? Is there a clear path to profitability?
- **Feasibility**: Do you have the resources, or can you acquire them, to bring this idea to life?
- **Impact**: Does this idea contribute positively to your intended audience or community? Will anyone care? What pain will it reduce, or pleasure will it increase?

For now, we want to focus on this exercise's high-level output. Once you determine the final idea, we will break down all these components and scrutinize the business idea in great detail.

In conclusion, many exercises exist to help develop ideas for a successful business. An excellent place to start is looking at your passions or areas for which you are uniquely qualified. Then, walk through some of the techniques above and finally consider their viability. Once you have it locked in, we will take it to the next level and come up with the plan to make it a success: the business plan.

CHAPTER 4
PLAN YOUR WORK AND WORK YOUR PLAN—THE BUSINESS PLAN

Imagine you are driving in a deserted area. It's late; you are tired and have never been here before. The GPS on your phone stops working due to no cell service. You are running low on gas. You look around and tell yourself this is no place to be stranded. You come to a fork in the road, but you have no idea which way to go. Should I go left? Should I go straight? Should I go right? Anxiety creeps in. This feels like a life-or-death situation.

You look in the glove compartment of your car, and voila, a map! In this scenario, a map becomes a lifeline, a detailed guide that provides direction and insights into the roads ahead. This analogy mirrors the role of a business plan in the entrepreneurial landscape. It acts as a comprehensive map that outlines the route, anticipates hurdles, and strategizes the journey toward creating a successful business. A well-crafted business plan also does much more; it communicates your vision, can potentially persuade investors, and serves as a constant reference point as your business evolves.

In the first chapter, we discussed crafting your version of the "down-and-dirty" business plan to validate the feasibility of your idea. Now that you have decided to take it to the next step, you will want to develop a more thorough business plan with specific details about what you will do and how you will do it. As the adage goes, "Fail to plan, plan to fail."

In business, I am a big fan of thinking about and documenting everything as much as possible before you do it. Then, when you get out onto the battlefield, and the shots start firing, everything will not seem so intense; you will have already prepared for it and can adjust much more efficiently and effectively.

In this chapter, we will look at all the distinct pieces of the business plan, and I will add any color that I think will be helpful for you when you create yours. Further, as an appendix to the book, I have included a copy of my company's business plan should you want to see what it looked like. Let's break down the components of the business plan now.

EXECUTIVE SUMMARY

The business plan begins with an executive summary, a concise overview that captures the essence of your business and its aspirations. It should include the business name, location, products or services offered, mission statement, and the business's purpose.

All in all, this section doesn't have to be overly complicated. Just write down the basics of what you are trying to achieve and attempt to break it down simply. Consider what you would say to people if they ask what your business does or what your "elevator pitch" is. If you have never heard of that term, it's a standard sales term that explains what your company does or what you are selling in the time it takes to ride on an elevator.

COMPANY DESCRIPTION

This section provides detailed information about the business, including its legal structure, initial ownership, history, nature, and the needs or demands it will fulfill within the market. Here, you want to break down more of the company's specifics, which are more tailored to the who and how.

PRODUCTS OR SERVICES

A detailed description of the products or services offered, including benefits to customers and the current development stage. This is pretty self-explanatory because it's essentially what you're selling. If you have multiple products or offerings, break them down into different categories. You will want to key in on what the product solves for the customer and use plain language. In general, with the business plan, you want to avoid jargon or industry language. You want to make it appeal to a mass audience, and simplicity is key.

MARKET ANALYSIS AND STRATEGY

Market analysis delves into the heart of the market you will serve, examining industry trends, target market segments, market sizing, and how you will attack the opportunity. For the market analysis, you can use the internet to research industry data points, such as current sizing and potential compounded annual growth rate (CAGR) estimates. Additionally, there are many third-party analyst reports on industries you might be able to access to help with sizing. For example, I used reports from Gartner, a research and consulting firm, to aid me in this process.

FINANCIAL PLAN

Financial projections for your company serve as a reality check, testing the feasibility of your business model against the rigor of numbers. Start with revenue projections, estimating sales based on market analysis, marketing strategies, and any unique industry knowledge. This step requires a balance of optimism and realism, ensuring projections are ambitious yet achievable.

I get that predicting your revenue will be incredibly difficult. If everyone could do this accurately, new businesses would have a one hundred percent success rate. Imagine how great it would be if you knew exactly how much money would come in! But you can't, and you won't. So give it your best guesstimate and back it up with data. You will have to be able to defend whatever you come up with.

Ironically, the number I came up with was $1.1 million, which was close to what we did in the first year. I used my sales at the company from the previous five years plus industry trends as my litmus test. Once I came up with those numbers, I moved it down twenty-five percent to be conservative. You will want this section to be specific and break down the revenue projections for your different categories, if applicable. For example, you can see my breakdowns in the appendix.

EXPENSE ESTIMATES

So now that you have a realistic gauge of your revenue projections (i.e., money coming in), you need to look at expenses (i.e., money going out). We don't need to overcomplicate things. It's really that simple. A company is really about money coming in and going out. Money coming in is less in your control, but money going out is. Therefore, initially, it is mission-critical to keep expenses down—like way, way, way, way down.

When evaluating expenses, we need to categorize them into one-time startup and ongoing operational expenses. These costs will clarify the financial commitment required to launch and sustain the business. The list of these expenses can be extensive. I included a list of the typical startup one-time and ongoing expenses in the appendix for you to reference when you are ready to put it together.

COMPETITIVE ANALYSIS

This section strategically outlines the competitive environment, focusing on direct competitors and their characteristics. It also defines your new company's strategic approach to establishing a competitive edge by exploiting gaps in the offerings of existing players. When analyzing your competitors and the competitive landscape, it is helpful to use a SWOT analysis. A SWOT analysis is where you identify your and your competitors' strengths, weaknesses, opportunities, and threats. When you go through this exercise, be realistic with yourself. How strong are your strengths really? What are your realistic weaknesses? Do honest self-reflection and be a harsh critic here. It will only help. You can see my example in the appendix.

MARKETING AND SALES STRATEGY

The marketing and sales strategy section outlines your company's initial marketing and sales plan, including pricing, sales tactics, advertising, promotions, and distribution strategies. In later chapters, we will discuss advanced marketing and sales strategies, but for now, let's focus on the basics. The marketing and sales strategy closely aligns with the market analysis section. Once we have a good understanding of our company's strengths and weaknesses, we can come up with a day-to-day game plan on how to attack them.

Let's break down the various components of the sales and marketing strategy. I will also provide examples of what mine looked like.

- **Develop a Unique Selling Proposition (USP):** A USP separates your company from the rest. This can't be fluff, either. You can't say, "We will provide the highest quality products and services." Everyone says that. You have to look at what makes your company unique. And once you do that, you can highlight the unique benefits of the product or service that differentiate it from competitors. You always want to position it from the value perspective OF THE CUSTOMERS. At the end of the day, the customers don't give a shit about you; they only care about what you can do for them.
- **Marketing Goals:** It is good to create some initial marketing goals for your first year. Your marketing goals will become much larger as you go, but in the beginning, you are just really trying to get your name out there. Marketing is not about closing deals; its really just making sure people know your company exists.

- **Marketing Strategies:** Marketing strategies are the platforms you can use to help get the word out. We will talk more about this in the Marketing 101 chapter.
- **Sales Strategy:** We will discuss more specifics about sales tactics and sales strategy in a later chapter, but for now, focus on year one.
  - **Sales Channels:** In this area, outline any "direct" (you and your employees) and "indirect" (distributors, partners, wholesalers) sales channels. Depending on the type of business you are creating, indirect might not be a viable option for year one.
  - **Sales Team:** This one is easy. Who is essentially going to be responsible for selling in your company? If you are starting a company by yourself, as I did, then congratulations! You already know who your sales team is—it's you! So get off your ass and sell something already, would you? Obviously, if you are starting a business with partners, identify who will be mainly responsible for sales and develop an initial plan for when and how you will build a sales team.
- **Partnerships and Collaborations:** Identify any companies that might want to work with you and with whom you can mutually support each other's causes. We will discuss this in great detail how to do this in the sales chapter.
- **Budget and Resource Allocation:** When considering all of these strategies, of course, you will want to determine how much to spend and where. You will want to document that in your business plan.
- **Monitoring and Evaluation:** You will want to document how you will track marketing activities and return on investment on this spend. You will want to develop key performance indicators (KPIs) for each marketing and sales activity. In the beginning, this doesn't need to be complicated; sometimes, a gut feeling will be all you have to go on if something works. However, you want metrics to help you make an informed decision about whether these activities are worth the investment.

- As an example for my company, the main KPI I looked at for sales and marketing was my travel expenses. There was a direct correlation between travel and corresponding sales. Travel expenses were easy to categorize in my accounting system, to track on a monthly or quarterly basis, and to tie directly to any sold deals or new opportunities created. Based on this information, I knew if I needed to ramp up or push back on travel.

Without an initial sales and marketing strategy, you are doomed for failure. This has to be one of your primary areas of focus. Once again, a business is just money coming in and money going out. Sales and marketing will determine the cash coming in, so don't shortchange this area. As you grow, both of these plans will change, but for now, as the adage goes, use the KISS methodology (Keep It Simple, Stupid), and you can adapt as you go.

MANAGEMENT TEAM AND ORGANIZATION

This area of the business plan is straightforward. You will want to profile the business' leadership team, as well as their role and experiences (that would be valuable to the customer or potential investors). Further, an organizational chart can help show the business's management hierarchy and can be incredibly helpful in assisting people to understand their roles. Especially for small organizations, everyone will "wear multiple hats," meaning they don't have just one job. But this can also lead to confusion about who's on first and what is on second. So even though people will wear multiple hats, it has to be abundantly clear who is responsible for what, or people will step on each other's toes and become resentful. If you need an example org chart, many are available for free online, or you can create them in Microsoft PowerPoint and other productivity apps.

OPERATIONAL PLAN

This area of the business plan details the business's physical location, facilities, equipment, labor, supply chains, and internal processes. It also includes any operational challenges and strategies for addressing them. Depending on the type of business you are starting, this can be incredibly complex or really simple. Regardless of the complexity, you need to document the operational plan to the best of your ability and any potential changes to it in year one that need to be considered ahead of time. As your organization grows, the operational plan will become crucial to your ability to scale the business. It will probably even necessitate an employee dedicated to it. I did this myself when I hired a COO or Chief Operating Officer, whose job is to look internally at the company, identify bottlenecks and opportunities, and prime the company for future growth.

ADAPTING YOUR PLAN FOR DIFFERENT AUDIENCES

Finally, a business plan is a dialogue tailored to resonate with its intended audience. And this audience varies. For most of the above, I discussed the business plan for your audience of you and the benefit of having a plan that you can work on. Although the plan can be for yourself, it can also be for investors or lenders if you decide to go that route. In a later chapter, we will discuss how to get inside the minds of these prospective partners and strategies to modify the business plan for those audiences.

Remember that when embarking on creating your business plan, it reflects your vision, a growth strategy, and your blueprint for success. Beyond your time and effort, it also demands your passion, insight, and commitment. As you navigate the intricacies of planning your business, let this guide serve as your map, pointing you toward where you should take the various forks on the road. As always, "plan your work and then work your plan."

CHAPTER 5
FUNDING YOUR BUSINESS

> *Cash rules everything around me, C.R.E.A.M, get the money. Dollar dollar bill, y'all.*
>
> WU-TANG CLAN

Ok, we have done it. We have gone through the necessary work to develop the business plan. We now have the directions and the map to success and are ready to start. We are pumped! But one thing stands in our way. In the immortal words of the character Blond Treehorn Thug," "Where's the money, Lebowski?" So, I ask you the same question: Where's the money, Lebowski? Yes, cash, cold hard cash. That fickle bitch, and the vital artery of every company.

I understand that the folks reading this book will be all over the map regarding your current financial situation. I am here to tell you that it is ok. There are many different ways to fund your business, and a little creativity can go a long way. In this chapter, I will break down the various options and talk about the pros and cons of each. Funding a business can seem daunting, but it doesn't need to be. I remember having a lot of anxiety about how I was going to going to fund the company. The best advice I can give you is to take a deep breath and explore all the options. One will present itself, and once it does, seize it and move forward. Let's look at your options to kick off your funding journey.

Here are the options we will explore for funding a business:

1. Bootstrapping
2. Raising capital via angel investors and VCs
3. Crowdfunding
4. Exploring small business grants and loans

OPTION 1: BOOTSTRAPPING YOUR BUSINESS

The term "bootstrapping" originally comes from the phrase "pulling oneself up by one's bootstraps," which means to improve one's situation by one's own efforts, without any outside help. In a business context, bootstrapping involves starting and growing a business using your own resources without external investment or minimal borrowing. It's essentially a method that echoes the age-old adage, "Make do with what you have."

This approach has its roots in the concept of self-sufficiency and self-discipline, offering you complete control over your business but also placing the burden of financial risk squarely on your shoulders. The benefits are clear: Your ownership remains undiluted, you can make all decisions swiftly without investor input, and the business can grow at a pace that matches its actual, organic progress. The challenges, however, are just as real: Limited resources mean every decision carries weight, and growth can be slower, requiring patience and a long-term perspective.

For me, I decided to bootstrap my business. I did this for two reasons: First, my whole journey was about controlling my future. I didn't want to depend on or be beholden to anyone because it went against my overall goals and principles. Additionally, I told myself that if the business could not stand on its own two feet, it probably wasn't going to be successful in the long run, and then what was the point anyway? When thinking through decisions, make sure your principles are your guiding light.

Bootstrapping Examples

The bootstrapping approach not only worked for my company but has also worked for many others. Let's look at a few:

GoPro: Nick Woodman founded GoPro using his savings and money borrowed from his parents. The company grew organically through reinvestment of its earnings and exploded in popularity, leading to a highly successful initial public offering (IPO) in 2014.

Spanx: Sara Blakely started Spanx with $5,000 in savings and used her credit card to fund the initial operations. She had no outside investment and managed to build her business from scratch. Blakely eventually turned Spanx into a billion-dollar brand without significant outside investment.

Patagonia: Yvon Chouinard started Patagonia by initially selling climbing gear he made himself. He funded the early stages of his business using personal savings and income from his small blacksmith business.

I had a buddy of mine use a credit card and take a cash advance from it to buy his first rental property and start a real estate investment business. Five years later, he had around eighty investment properties and was generating over half a million dollars in profit annually, not including the appreciation of his properties. So, it just goes to show that you can have a thriving company without a lot of initial capital.

Initially Funding the Bootstrapping Company

There are multiple ways to initially self-fund the bootstrapped company. For example, like in the examples above, you can take money out of your savings, borrow money from parents or loved ones, or use credit cards. There is another creative option available, and it is something I have never heard about in any of the "starting a business" books I read: taking funds out of your 401k and using that to self-fund the company. This is what I did. Let's look at how to do it now.

Through the last chapter's exercises, we should now know how much anticipated capital we will need. When I went through my process, I came up with an anticipated amount I would need to fund the company, and then I looked at what assets I had at my disposal. Outside of the equity in my home, my only real assets were around $75,000 in cash, which we discussed I had already targeted to use for my personal expenses, and roughly $75,000 in a 401k.

I remember wondering if I could somehow use that money in my 401k for the business, like taking out a loan or some other way. A big part of being a successful entrepreneur is not taking no for an answer and being resourceful. Some simple web searching identified that I could! This changed everything for me. It was a complete lightbulb moment and inflection point for me, which made the business a reality.

So what is it? The approach to using these funds to fund the business is a government program commonly known as Rollovers as Business Startups (ROBS). This arrangement lets you invest your retirement funds into a new or existing business without incurring early withdrawal penalties or taxes.

ROBS can be a powerful way to fund a business without traditional loans or external capital. Still, it does come with significant responsibilities and some risks. The main risk is that you can lose all the money, which at that point was my entire retirement savings if the company fails. But as we discussed, I couldn't touch the money in my 401k until I was sixty, and what better way to invest it than to invest in myself?

Also, it does come with significant responsibilities. If you decide to go this route, it is critical to consult with financial advisors and legal experts specializing in ROBS arrangements to ensure compliance and assess the suitability of this funding option for your situation. I hired a company, Guidant Financial, to handle the whole process and ensure my company met the requirements. It was well worth the money I spent to do so. I included some additional information about ROBS in an appendix at the end of the book if you want to know more specifics about the process and what type of companies typically use this unique structure.

Funding your company via the bootstrapped model is usually the path of least resistance for many entrepreneurs, which is why it is so popular. Although there are some downsides to the bootstrapped company, this approach does ensure a strong foundation is laid: one that supports sustainable growth, preserves your equity, and maintains the entrepreneurial spirit at the heart of the venture.

While bootstrapping is a great option for many, it might not be for everyone. Let's look at the other options.

OPTION 2: RAISING CAPITAL VIA ANGEL INVESTORS AND VCS

Let's say you don't have the resources to bootstrap or are generally ok with giving up some control for the stability of having more capital initially. Consider angel investment or venture capital (VC) investment. Many companies have successfully used this route to fund their companies and have had great success.

Before we go into it, the following is to be used as a primer and high-level overview for your consideration. Raising capital via one of these approaches is a whole book in itself, and the landscape changes rapidly. Many specialized books and other resources can help you illuminate how to understand their motivations, identify specific angel investors or VC companies, craft your pitch, and develop strategies to close the deal.

But from a high-level perspective, let's first look at the difference between these two different avenues and the individual motivations for these two types of investors. Angel investors and venture capitalists, while both motivated by the prospect of returns, operate under very different paradigms.

Angel investors, often individuals investing their own capital, are drawn to early-stage ventures, motivated by potential financial returns and personal satisfaction in being involved and helping guide startups.

They tend to invest smaller amounts and may offer valuable mentorship based on their own entrepreneurial experiences. I am an angel investor and have invested in a few local businesses that friends have started, as well as some early-stage tech companies through AngelList. I relished the opportunity to help, provide advice (if they wanted it), and be a part of their journey. As I have been through my journey and seen the outsized returns possible, I categorize these investments into the "high risk" section of my overall financial portfolio. I know that many of my angel investors friends look at it the same way.

Angel Investing and VC Examples

There have been many instances of successful companies that have used angel investing to fund their business. One of the most famous examples is **Google**. Google received its first significant funding from angel investors, including Andy Bechtolsheim, co-founder of Sun Microsystems, who wrote a check for $100,000 in 1998. This initial investment was critical in helping Google scale its infrastructure and expand its operations during its early days. Spoiler alert: That investment wound up working out for Andy. Don't believe me? Just Google it. See what I did there? I am so clever, aren't I? Wait, don't answer that.

Another example is **WhatsApp.** This globally popular messaging app received its initial funding from a group of angel investors, including former employees of Yahoo. The seed funding helped it grow without ads. Eventually, it led to its acquisition by Facebook in 2014 for approximately $19 billion, making it one of the largest tech acquisitions at the time. For the angels who invested, that's what's up.

In contrast, VCs are fully operating businesses themselves. They are investment firms that specifically provide funding to startups and early-stage companies with high growth potential. They manage pooled funds of money with a mandate to minimize risk and maximize returns over a defined period. They are drawn to startups with proven traction and teams, scalable business models, and a clear path to significant growth and eventual exit.

On the VC route, many successful companies have also used this path to fund their business, including **Facebook (now Meta Platforms Inc.)**. Several rounds of venture capital fueled Facebook's rise to global dominance in social media. One of its earliest investments came from Accel Partners, which invested $12.7 million in 2005 when Facebook was just stretching beyond the college market. This investment was critical for Facebook's expansion and, ultimately, its dominance in social networking. I am sure Accel made a lot of "friends" out of their backers with this investment. They liked it … a lot. Thumbs up! You can't handle this level of humor, can you? It's just too damn clever.

Another example is **Amazon:** Before becoming the e-commerce titan it is today, Amazon secured a $8 million investment from Kleiner Perkins Caufield & Byers in 1995. This early infusion of venture capital helped Amazon rapidly scale its operations, expand its inventory, and build out its distribution network, paving the way for its current status as a global retail giant. Hey Alexa, did that investment work out for the VC firm? "Yes, that was a Prime return for Kleiner Perkins Caufield & Byer." Man, I am on fire! Do the jokes ever begin?

Understanding Investor Expectations

Understanding the motivations and putting yourself in the shoes of why an angel or VC would invest in your company is crucial in tailoring your pitch to address specific investor concerns. For angels, emphasizing the product's potential and the team's personal drive can be more persuasive. In contrast, VCs require a strong focus on market size, growth potential, and evidence of traction, reassured by data-driven projections and a clear exit strategy.

If this option seems attractive to you, seek out additional resources that can help guide you on this path.

OPTION 3: CROWDFUNDING

Does bootstrapping or the angel/VC approach not sound appealing? Let's look at crowdfunding. Crowdfunding is a method of raising capital through a large number of individuals, typically via online platforms such as Kickstarter. This approach taps into the vast networks of people, mainly online via social media and crowdfunding websites, to bring investors and entrepreneurs together.

The allure and popularity of crowdfunding to raise capital for business ventures have significantly magnified in the Digital Age. This method presents a dual opportunity to secure funding and validate the market's appetite for your product or service. It allows you to appeal directly to your future customers and advocates and offer them a stake in the project's success.

Likewise, with angels and VCs, this option to fund your business can be advantageous but also highly nuanced. The choice of platform, crafting of the campaign, engagement with backers, and fulfillment of promises post-campaign become pivotal elements in this intricate dance of expectation, persuasion, and delivery. The full spectrum of steps to take here is outside the scope of this book, and should you consider this a viable option, you will want to hear directly from experts on the best path to take.

Crowdfunding Examples

However, there are many examples of crowdfunding success stories. This form of funding seems particularly successful for companies focused on a single product. Take, for instance, **Pebble Technology**. Pebble started as one of Kickstarter's most famous success stories. The company developed the Pebble Smartwatch, one of the first smartwatches that could connect to iOS and Android smartphones. Their Kickstarter campaign in 2012 raised over $10 million from nearly 69,000 backers, far exceeding the initial $100,000 goal. Fitbit eventually bought Pebble for tens of millions of dollars. DAMMNNN...that's a lot of pebbles! Its early crowdfunding success was monumental in the tech industry.

Another one that many of us are probably familiar with the product is **Oculus VR**. Oculus initiated a Kickstarter campaign in 2012 to fund the development of their Oculus Rift VR headset. The campaign raised $2.4 million, surpassing its $250,000 goal and helping to revive interest in virtual reality technology. Oculus was later acquired by Facebook (now Meta Platforms) for approximately $2 billion in 2014. Now, if I can just find a way to get my son to stop playing Gorilla Tag on the Oculus much, it's an odd sight to see happening in my kitchen.

OPTION 4: EXPLORING SMALL BUSINESS GRANTS AND LOANS

Ok, so maybe none of the above options sound good to you. Wow, you are picky, aren't you? Who hurt you? There are still other avenues to explore that can work with any of the options above. Small business grants and loans can be vital tools to fund your company. Although both serve the same goal of delivering capital to your business, each comes with its opportunities and challenges. Although I did not take on any of these approaches, I made myself aware of what was available, and exploring them for your business is a good idea.

Grants

Navigating grants unveils a world where funding, free from repayment obligations, is awarded based on merit, innovation, or alignment with specific objectives from the bodies who hand them out. Federal agencies, state governments, non-profit organizations, and corporate entities offer grants targeting various sectors, from technology and research to environmental conservation and social entrepreneurship. The allure of grants lies in their non-repayable nature (yes, you read that right, you don't have to pay it back) and the credibility and recognition they bestow upon recipients, elevating a business's stature right off the get-go. Yes, if you receive a grant you will be seen as a big deal and as very important, whether or not you have many leatherbound books and/or your apartment smells of rich mahogany.

The quest for grants involves a detailed application process, where proposals must demonstrate the innovation and potential impact of the business idea and align with the grantor's objectives. Crafting a compelling narrative that articulates the uniqueness of your proposition, supported by data-driven projections and a clear execution plan, is key. The process requires preparation, attention to detail in fulfilling every requirement, and adhering to submission deadlines. Networking with past recipients and engaging with grant-making bodies can offer invaluable insights into the nuances of a successful application.

I did some high-level research on what grants, if any, would apply to my situation. I determined that the length of time, effort, and know-how was more than I wanted to bite off, as I had so many other parts of the business to figure out. Additionally, the more I learned about it, the more it became clear to me that I would have to hire a company to handle the process, and the risk of spending that money with no guaranteed outcome wasn't for me.

An example of a company that took out a grant and turned it into success is **Honest Tea**. Honest Tea received a Small Business Innovation Research (SBIR) grant from the U.S. Department of Agriculture to help develop its products. They also secured a small business loan to start production. From there, Honest Tea grew into a leading organic tea brand. It was acquired by The Coca-Cola Company in 2011 for approximately $100 million. That was a Beau-TEA-ful outcome for them for sure. *Oh God, is he going to do this whole shtick again?*

Loans

Loans constitute a broad spectrum of financial products offered by banks, credit unions, and specialized lenders, including microloan organizations such as Kiva and online lending platforms such as LendingClub. These financial products range from traditional term loans, characterized by fixed interest rates and monthly repayment schedules, to lines of credit that offer flexible access to funds up to a specified limit.

Securing a business loan or line of credit will carry a scrutiny of creditworthiness as well as a scrutiny of your business plan. Lenders will seek assurance of repayment, so making a strong business plan presentation and solid financial projections will help you in a successful loan application. Personal credit scores, particularly for new businesses without an established credit history, play a significant role in determining eligibility and terms. Additionally, if you go this route, you will likely have to sign a personal guarantee, essentially an agreement that if the business does not pay the loan off, the lender can come after your personal assets, like your house. This stipulation is why I ultimately decided this route was not for me.

Grants and Loans Examples

Just because it wasn't for me doesn't mean it won't be for you. Many companies have used these approaches to help fund their business. Let's look at a few now.

Ben and Jerry's: The founders of Ben and Jerry's used a combination of personal savings and a $12,000 small business loan to open their first ice cream shop in a renovated gas station in Burlington, Vermont. The reward for Ben and Jerry taking on the risk of that loan was sweet and delicious! *Oh boy, here we go again. Hopefully, these lame puns will improve.*

TOMS Shoes: Blake Mycoskie used personal savings and a small business loan to start TOMS Shoes. The loan helped fund the initial production and launch of the company, which helped them become a powerhouse in the shoe industry. They used that loan to make sure those shoes were made for walking! *Oh wow, come on, Kevvie. You are better than that.*

Should you wish to continue researching whether loans or grants are right for funding your business, here is a list of resources to get you started.

- **Grants.gov**: A comprehensive database of federally funded grants, offering a searchable repository of opportunities across various sectors.
- **SBA.gov**: The Small Business Administration's site provides detailed information on SBA loans, microloans, and grant programs specifically designed for small businesses. SBA loans stand out and are attractive due to their favorable terms and lower interest rates. They are designed expressly to bolster the growth of small businesses.
- **SCORE.org**: Partnered with the SBA, SCORE offers free mentoring to small businesses and can provide guidance on financing options and application strategies.
- **SBDCs (Small Business Development Centers)**: Located nationwide, SBDCs offer free business consulting and low-cost training services, including assistance with financial planning and access to funding sources.
- **GrantWatch.com**: A subscription-based service aggregating grants from federal, state, local, and foundation sources, categorized by industry and region for easy navigation.

In conclusion, there are many ways to fund your company. Hugely successful companies have been built with each approach. An assessment of the inventory of your existing assets, honest risk tolerance around loans, and what level of control you are willing to give up in the beginning is an excellent way to start the consideration process. As such, in life, there are pros and cons to each approach. I suggest exploring all the options available to you. But rest assured, there is A ROUTE for you to fund your business and dream. I get that this seems like it could be an overwhelming roadblock, but I am here to tell you that it can be knocked down.

PHASE THREE
LAUNCH PHASE—THE BACK END PLUMBING

This next phase will dive into the less sexy but still instrumental aspects of starting and running a successful business. We will discuss choosing a business name, providing the options and pros and cons for the business' legal structure, legal requirements and registrations, and Accounting 101. For each of these individual components there are many other resources for you to read before making final decisions. However, my goal is to distill these areas down and simplify them for you, highlighting all the key components you need to understand. Sure, they are not as exciting areas of the business, but they are still critical while you are launching. Let's get into them now.

CHAPTER 6
CHOOSING A BUSINESS NAME

> *The name is a critical element for a company. It should evoke something about what the company does and be easy to remember.*
>
> ELON MUSK (CEO OF TESLA, SPACEX, NEUROLINK, TWITTER, AND PROBABLY 5 OTHER COMPANIES AFTER THIS BOOK HAS BEEN PUBLISHED)

Naming your company is a pivotal moment, a ceremonial rite that cements your business with identity and purpose and, if you're like me, fulfills a lifelong dream. This initial staking of the flag into the ground requires a blend of creativity and strategic foresight, ensuring the chosen name resonates with your market, yourself, and your team. Further, the name needs to pass smoothly through legal and digital checks. Let's dive into all that goes into choosing and protecting your company name now.

CHOOSING A BUSINESS NAME

This part is one of my favorite parts of creating a new company! As the old adage goes (yes, I like adages), "A name says it all." You want to craft a name that captures the essence of your business while remaining memorable to your audience and ideally serving as a motivational tool for yourself. When I started to think about naming my company, one of the most stimulating and helpful exercises I went through was one I read about in *The Toilet Paper Entrepreneur*. In it, there is a great section where he talks about writing down a list of the reasons why you are starting the company. Then, he mentions that many times, one of these reasons can become the eventual name of the company. He challenges the reader to come up with the REAL reasons they are starting the company. Beyond "to make more money," really get in touch with the emotional reasons why you are doing it. He challenges the reader to come up with reasons that would make you cry or get emotional thinking about it.

I wanted to start a company because I wanted to control my future. I am a control freak, but it is more about personal control, a.k.a. controlling myself and what I do with my life. I know I cannot control others or what happens in the world.

This desire for control stemmed from something that happened in my teenage years. Without diving too much into it (I will save it for a different book), when I was sixteen, one of my friends, Barrett Modisette, was brutally murdered by gunshot right in front of me and some friends. As you can imagine, this tragic event shook me to my core. At sixteen, I was brutally informed of the painful and sobering fact that life was short and that it was not promised to anyone.

For five years after that shooting, my life spiraled out of control. Let's look at the highlights: I had bad PTSD (post-traumatic stress disorder), which completely changed how I felt and acted from before. Shortly after the murder happened, I received death threats so I wouldn't testify. As such, I had to move states for a month. I had to change high schools mid-way through my junior year, and my friend group got majorly disrupted as a result. My family had no idea how to handle the situation or me, and I felt like an outsider in my own home. To feel safer, I decided to leave Illinois, the state I grew up in, and attend College in Colorado (SKO Buffs)—a place where I knew no one and was completely out of my comfort zone. So, quite simply, my life was way, way, way out of control. As I eventually came out of my PTSD and started to heal and get my life back on track, I made it my mission for the remainder of my days to control my life as best I could. I was maniacal about it and still am.

When I entered the workforce, I quickly realized that I was not in control of my career. Through the years, I have seen many talented people get fired or laid off for really poor reasons. At every job I had, I greatly exceeded my sales targets, but I NEVER felt safe. I always felt like I could be let go or fired at any point. So, my number one reason to start a business was to control my career. In one of my first meetings with Dan, he asked me, "Why do you want to start a company?" Without hesitation or thinking about it, I answered, "Control." He smiled.

So, when I went through this exercise to come up with my company name, I wrote down all the reasons I was doing it on paper. They included control, freedom, not relying on others, financial security, being my own boss, financial independence, retiring early, and doing what I want with my life. I then, as instructed, attempted to think of iterations for the company name based on all of those.

The one that stood out to me right away as the potential company name was the word "control." First and foremost, it was bold, which I liked. I thought to myself, *Fortune favors the bold.* But I also liked that part of our company's mission was to help companies control costs and electronic data. So, not only was it personally meaningful, but it was meaningful to my prospective customers. I can still remember where I was when I settled on it. I was on a train returning to my house from a meeting with Dan. This was the very meeting where he asked me why I wanted to start a company, and I said, "Control." I looked at my list and saw it was on there as well. Bam, that's it! I got it! I remember getting goosebumps. So yeah, look for the goosebump name.

Ultimately, I settled on "Controle," which was my personal goal in conjunction with what we were doing for the customer. I put an "E" at the end of the word control to signify electronic data. At the time, many companies and my eventual competitors in the eDiscovery market company names started with the letter "E." I always like doing things differently, so I put the "E" at the end instead of the beginning (i.e., I didn't call it "eControl"). Later on, we would get many jokes from our customers that we must be a Spanish-speaking company because *controle* is Spanish for "control," and even though we pronounced the company like the word control, many people would say "Control-e" when they first were introduced to us. Regardless, it was a successful name, and I received many compliments on it during our reign. It stood out. The fact that it was tied to a common word people would hear in everyday life also helped. Still, to this day, when anyone says the word "control," I smirk.

So, here is your challenge: Figure out WHY you are doing this. What are the emotional reasons you are doing it? Be honest. If you are embarrassed about why you are doing it, don't worry. You don't need to share this list with anyone. Maybe you want to impress your ex or stick it to that teacher who said you wouldn't amount to anything. It doesn't matter; just be honest. Then, look at how you could match your offerings to those goals. It was exceptionally motivating that my goal was the company name. It stared me in the face every day for the decade I ran the company.

Whenever shit got hard, or I felt frustrated, my company name reminded me why I was doing it. And I am proud to say that I accomplished my goal. A decade after I started the company and sold it for the second time (more on this later), I had made enough money that I was able to retire at forty-five and truly take control of my life. No one can tell me to do shit, and I can't tell you how valuable that is to me. So, make the company name meaningful. It will want to make you get up and fight every day, and there will be many days where you will have to fight.

NAME AVAILABILITY CHECKS

Once a list of potential names or a name crystallizes, a critical step is ensuring your chosen name doesn't infringe upon existing trademarks or business registrations. I remember being so excited when I came up with Controle and then simultaneously becoming terrified that it might already be in use. You will have to check multiple different levels of these business registrations, starting at the state level where your business will operate.

Most state governments offer online databases where you can search registered business names, providing an immediate filter for potential conflicts. Then, you will expand the search to the federal level, particularly the United States Patent and Trademark Office (USPTO), which offers a broader view, identifying any national claims to your proposed names. This dual-level check mitigates the risk of legal complications that could derail your efforts and necessitate a costly rebranding down the line.

If you choose a company like LegalZoom to do the incorporation, they will do these searches for you. Luckily for me, no businesses under the name Controle or with the word Controle in it were in the same line of business. Perfect. Now, on to securing and protecting the domain.

SECURING A DOMAIN NAME

In today's digital-first marketplace, securing an online domain that matches your business name is a necessity. This digital real estate becomes the primary gateway through which customers engage with your company.

Finding availability for a domain name is easy. Domain registers like GoDaddy and others provide a platform to search for available domain names, instantly revealing the landscape of possibilities. Typically, you will want to favor the ".com" extension for its universal recognition and trustworthiness among consumers. Just ask yourself how comfortable you would be purchasing something from a ".com" extension versus ".biz." Exactly. Your customers will think the same.

When a direct match to your business name is unavailable, you will have to get creative. Adding simple prefixes or suffixes without diluting the brand identity can unearth options that remain intuitive to your audience. Once identified, swiftly acquiring your domain name is important, as the dynamic nature of the Internet means availability can change rapidly.

I used GoDaddy to conduct my search. Once I decided upon the company name and did the various searches to ensure it wasn't used by someone else in my industry, I held my breath as I typed in controle.com. Instantly, I got a result back. It read, "Sorry, this domain is already in use." SHIT! Don't be surprised if this happens to you. As of writing this in 2024, there are gazillions (yes, I said it) of websites on the web. And many people buy domains to resell them (this is a big business). But it is what it is; don't sweat the stuff you can't control. Since controle.com was taken, I eventually decided to go with take-controle.com. It wasn't as ideal as controle.com (a manufacturing parts company website in Spanish), but it would do. The only challenge with having a company name different from the website is that people WILL call your company name whatever the domain is. I often would have new salespeople at our partners or customers call us "Take Controle." One of my personal favorites is when an EMC salesperson introduced me to their customer as "Kevin from Totally in Control." I didn't even correct her. It made me giggle out loud, but I just went with it.

I know this confusing "different-domain-versus-company-name" dilemma also happened to my mentor, Dan. His website was thinkahead.com, but the company's name was Ahead. People used to call them "Think Ahead" all the time. It's not a problem; it's just more annoying than anything. So, attempt to have the domain as close to your company name as possible. As organizations grow, they will often procure the domain they always wanted from the company that owns it. I tried contacting the Controle.com people but never got a response. Dan eventually got ahead.com, which serves as his website today. Check them out. They are a great company.

Even with this book, I went to secure a new domain name so I could use it to answer any of your questions. Theblueprint.com was taken. Damnit. There were other options, such as blueprint.biz, but again, go with ".com" if possible. I settled on itstheblueprint.com.

Random side note: If you want to see a funny clip about the lack of domains available, search up "www.clownpenis.fart SNL skit," a Saturday Night Live skit that shows a fictional financial services firm that waited too long to get a domain, and the last one available is www.clownpenis.fart. Hilarious.

Now that we have secured our domain, let's protect our chosen company name.

PROTECTING YOUR BRAND NAME

With your business name and domain secured, the final fortress to erect is the trademark, a legal safeguard that protects your company name from unauthorized use. While somewhat complicated, this process fortifies your market position, granting you exclusive rights to use the name in connection with your goods or services. We will discuss this in further detail in the IP section, so we will save this process for later.

In conclusion, when thinking of your company name, make it meaningful to your customers and, ideally, yourself. This name will stare you in the face every day, so make sure you take the time to consider it thoughtfully. Once you decide, secure your domain rights and trademark the name. Now that we have our name, let's figure out our legal structure.

CHAPTER 7
CHOOSING THE PROPER BUSINESS STRUCTURE

Understanding the foundation upon which the back end of a business is built begins with exploring the legal structures available to you. Initially, this decision could seem as if it is just administrative, but as you will see, that's not the case. The structure you choose will underpin your business's operational, financial, and legal foundation and influence everything from personal liability, exposure to tax obligations, and the ability to attract investment. The spectrum of options, such as sole proprietorship, partnership, limited liability companies (LLC), and corporations, can be confusing at first. But once you get into it, you will realize it's not all that daunting, and usually, your choice becomes clear, as it did for me.

After reading this segment, if you are still confused or unclear, you can further educate yourself. Further, I am NOT an attorney or accountant, so don't take any of the following as legal or tax advice. There are plenty of accountants and attorneys out there who can aid you in this process if you need it.

Additionally, another good idea to help you decide is to chat with any of the entrepreneurs you interviewed in the beginning or anyone you know with experience in this area. I did this, and I found it helpful in my decision-making process.

Let's break down the options now.

SOLE PROPRIETORSHIP

Sole proprietorships represent the most straightforward form of business structure. They are essentially one-person operations where the distinction between the owner (you) and the business is virtually nonexistent. These structures are easy to set up, generally have lower costs to create, and operate with minimal regulatory requirements.

This simplicity, however, carries with it personal liability, as debts and legal obligations you take on for the business become your debts and obligations personally, which is not ideal for many reasons. Ideally, you want a separation between personal and business obligations.

In this structure, taxation is equally simple, with profits and losses flowing through to the owner's personal tax return. This process is known as pass-through taxation, which avoids the complexity of dealing with corporate tax rates but also mingles business finances with personal tax obligations and potentially can lead to you paying unnecessary or higher taxes.

The types of businesses that commonly have this structure include freelancers and consultants, home-based businesses (like eBay sellers), in-home contractors like plumbers and electricians, and independent contractors in the gig economy (like Uber drivers and Grubhub delivery personnel).

PARTNERSHIPS

Before we get into the legal structures of partnerships, I feel compelled to add a personal note on business partnerships—not the legal structure, but going into business with someone. First off, know that they are exceptionally difficult to maintain, more so than you could imagine. No matter how well you think you know someone, money complicates things, and egos can, and most likely will, get in the way. I know many people, myself included, who have been burned in a myriad of ways by a partner they thought would be great, only to have things turn out differently than expected.

Another wrinkle to consider for potential conflict when going into business with someone is how profits will be split up versus who is actually bringing in the money. The legal structure of a partnership has clear rules on how money will be divided. However, just know there is a real likelihood for one partner to carry more weight than the other but have to split the profits anyway. I witnessed this firsthand when a friend had a two-person law firm but was doing ninety percent of the work for fifty percent of the profits. It got so bad that the other partner clearly knew what was happening but didn't care, letting my friend continue doing all the work. And they were close friends. It became a real daily stressor for my buddy and eventually led to a business divorce.

I can tell you that I have met many business owners. In the vast majority (I would say close to eighty percent) of those I have met who had business partners, it didn't work out and eventually led to them splitting. Many times, a business divorce can be just as messy or even worse than a marriage. In some extreme cases, it can even take down a company. So be extremely careful here.

Now, this doesn't always happen; there are certainly stories of successful partnerships. But just being aware of it will set you up better for success in communication and structuring legal agreements to protect you. But now, let's look at the legal structure of partnerships.

Partnerships encompass various sub-forms, such as general partnerships, limited partnerships, and limited liability partnerships, and extend the principled ideas of sole proprietorship but now to a collection of individuals. The idea is for business partners to pool their financial resources, expertise, and skills, which can then help the business grow and succeed. Additionally, in theory, partners can then share the responsibilities and workload, making managing the business easier and more efficient for all involved.

These structures maintain pass-through taxation but also introduce the dynamics and complications of shared responsibility and decision-making. Additionally, unlike sole proprietorships, more work must be performed upfront to establish a partnership agreement detailing the business's functions around key areas such as decision-making and profit sharing. This cannot be ignored due to what I mentioned above.

Liability, however, remains a pivotal concern, particularly in general partnerships where each partner is jointly and severally liable for the partnership's debts and obligations. This factor requires thorough trust and alignment among partners. So, what does that mean? If your partner does something stupid and your company gets sued, well, that is your problem as much as theirs. Does that sound like fun?

Businesses that commonly have this type of structure include professional service firms like law and accounting firms, real estate development companies, venture capital businesses, and healthcare practices such as group medical and dental practices.

LIMITED LIABILITY CORPORATION, OR LLC FOR SHORT

The advent of the limited liability company, or LLC, offers a bridge between the simplicity of sole proprietorships and partnerships but also adds an element of lowering personal risks by leveraging the protective veil of corporations. LLCs afford owners, typically called members, protection from personal liability, insulating your personal assets from business debts and claims. This is HUGE.

Additionally, this structure retains the tax benefits of pass-through taxation while offering flexibility in management and operation, detailed through an operating agreement. This flexibility of operations, simplified taxation, and legal protections appeal to entrepreneurs seeking protection without all the formalities of a corporation. On the downside, startup costs to create an LLC are higher, and annual dues are associated with maintaining the LLC. Additionally, depending on your situation, you may need to hire a law firm to help create the operating agreement, which could further exasperate startup costs.

My experience with my entrepreneur friends is that most of the time, the LLC is decided on as the entity of choice. And this is a continuing trend. According to the National Association of Small Business

(NSBA), as of recent years, around **thirty-five to fifty percent** of small businesses in the United States operate as LLCs.

Initially, due to requirements for the ROBS program I used to fund the company, I started Controle as a C corporation. However, in our second year of business, we decided to change and operate as an LLC going forward due to the advantages I discussed above. We started a new company known as Controle, LLC. This was the entity we eventually sold and remained the entity after we merged with our acquiring company to the final sale and exit.

Not only did I choose the LLC for our ultimate structure, but it has also become the entity of choice for me for other businesses I have started and have to this day. As of the writing of this book, I have four other LLCs. Two of them are for vacation destination rental properties that I own, one in Siesta Key, Florida, voted the number-one beach in the USA many times over, and a lake house in beautiful Elkhorn, Wisconsin, about ninety minutes from my personal residence in Chicagoland.

If you are curious and want to see what eventually selling your company can afford you, you can see both here. And please rent them! You, too, can live that Kevvie life here:

Siesta Key, Florida, condo on the beach: https://bit.ly/BlueprintBeachProperty

Lakehouse ninety minutes from Chicagoland: https://bit.ly/BlueprintLakeProperty

And yes, if you are wondering, yes, I am aware I am a shameless self-promoting whore. You can take the guy out of sales but not the sales out of the guy.

Further, I have a film production company (more on this later) and a book publishing company (that is producing this book, and the proceeds from this book will go into it). I chose an LLC for both of them for all the reasons I discussed above.

Finally, the types of businesses that choose LLCs overlap with businesses that choose partnerships but also expand beyond those. They include professional services firms such as law and accounting firms, rental property owners such as myself, retail and e-commerce stores, technology startups (Dan chose an LLC for Ahead), and a slew of other businesses.

C OR S CORPORATION

Corporations, encompassing C corporations and S corporations, are the most complex business structures. They are characterized by their distinct legal identity, which is separate from their owners. This separation shields owners from personal liability, creating a fortress safeguarding personal assets from business liabilities.

The major challenge with C corporations is that they face the dreaded "double taxation," where taxes are levied first on corporate profits and then again on dividends to its shareholders, a.k.a. you. Since you are the owner of the C corporation stock and are getting paid by the corporation, you are getting taxed twice. Seems like a great deal, right? This double taxation is a significant consideration for those contemplating this structure.

The types of businesses that commonly have a C Corp structure are larger, especially those that plan to issue stock, attract venture capital, or eventually go public. Many of the most well-known publicly held companies use this structure because they need to issue stock to the public and need it to benefit from the structure's ability to accommodate a large number of shareholders. I am sure many of you are shareholders in one or many of the companies below, and the C Corp structure allows for this. Here are some quick lists: In tech, we have Apple, Inc., Microsoft Corporation, and Amazon.com, Inc. In healthcare, there's Pfizer, Inc. and Johnson and Johnson, Inc. In retail and consumer goods, there's Walmart, Inc. and The Coca-Cola Company. Anyway, you get the gist.

S corporations, by contrast, employ many of the same protections as C corporations. However, a major difference is that they enjoy pass-through taxation, a privilege granted to entities meeting specific Internal Revenue Service (IRS) criteria. This allows them to combine liability protection with much more favorable tax treatment. So, most of the time, when I have seen my entrepreneur friends want to go the corporation route, they have chosen an S corporation.

The types of businesses that commonly have an S Corp structure are similar to those that would alternatively choose an LLC, such as professional service firms, small and family-owned businesses such as retail shops or restaurants, healthcare practices, and construction and contracting companies.

Once again, I know choosing the proper structure can feel overwhelming. But make no mistake: Some proper exploration and education into this space will pay off in terms of flexibility in managing the business, lowering taxes, and providing legal protections. Each business is different, and entrepreneurs have different risk tolerances. If you are still unsure about your path after reading this, speaking to an accountant or legal advisor is an excellent place to start.

CHAPTER 8
LEGAL REQUIREMENTS AND REGISTRATIONS 101—A CHECKLIST FOR THE NEW BUSINESS

If the prospects of establishing a business structure were not titillating enough for you, now we get to dive into an even more exciting topic: legal requirements, registrations, and permits. WOOHOO! YAY FOR US! In all seriousness, starting a new business involves navigating and establishing various legal requirements, registrations, and potential permits. Understanding and adhering to them is critical to ensure compliance and protect your business.

Now, this is probably the least of my favorite topics for starting a business and, frankly, something I recognized I was not good at, as I am generally unorganized regarding such matters. Because of this, I outsourced my understanding of what my business had to do to LegalZoom and various other tax and legal advisors. But to aid you in your process, I am including a checklist that provides a high-level overview of the essential items for most businesses. However, consult with legal and financial professionals to address the specific needs of your business and ensure you meet all regulatory requirements. Once again (yes, I know these disclaimers are annoying), I am not an attorney or accountant, so don't take this as legal or tax advice.

CHOOSE A BUSINESS STRUCTURE

- Make a final decision on the legal structure of your business (e.g., sole proprietorship, partnership, LLC, S corporation, or C corporation) that we discussed in the last chapter.
- Once you do, work with your advisors to understand the implications of each structure regarding liability, taxes, management, and annual filing dues and procedures.

REGISTER YOUR BUSINESS NAME

- Finalize your business name.
- Check for name availability with your state's business registration office and the USPTO to expand it to the federal level.
- Register the business name with the appropriate state agencies.

OBTAIN AN EMPLOYER IDENTIFICATION NUMBER (EIN)

- An Employer Identification Number (EIN) is a unique nine-digit number the IRS assigns to businesses for identification purposes. It is also known as a Federal Tax Identification Number.
- I always thought of an EIN as a business's social security number. You will use it often, and customers will ask for it when they set you up as a vendor in their system.
- Not every company will need an EIN, but most will, and you will likely need to.
- Apply online at the IRS website, by mail, fax (do fax machines seriously still exist?), or via the phone. Online applications are processed immediately, while mail and fax applications take longer. You can also use LegalZoom, as I have, or an accountant to handle it for you.

REGISTER FOR STATE AND LOCAL TAXES

- Register for state and local taxes, such as sales tax, usage tax, and employment taxes.
- If required, obtain a state tax identification number.
- It's a good idea to have an accountant or legal advisor help out when and where you will need to register with what states. We had employees in around ten states when we were done, and everyone outside of Illinois (where we were HQed) worked out of their house. Therefore, we had to register to do business in all these states. I learned that essentially if you have a physical location, which would include someone working out of their house, you have to register to do business in that state. This is called having a "nexus" in a state.

APPLY FOR NECESSARY LICENSES AND PERMITS

- Determine the licenses and permits required for your business at the federal, state, and local levels.
- Work with specialists and advisors in the industry you will serve to guide you in this area.
- Common licenses include general licenses required by most local governments to operate a business legally within a city or county, liquor licenses that sell alcohol such as bars, and professional licenses required for certain professions such as doctors, lawyers, and accountants.
- Common permits include zoning permits to ensure your business location complies with local zoning laws, health department permits for businesses that prepare and serve food, building permits for any construction or significant renovation of a business property, and sales tax permits which are required for companies that sell taxable goods or services (which is a whole ballyhoo in itself). Are we having fun yet?
- Apply for the necessary licenses and permits and renew them as required.

DRAFT AND FILE FORMATION DOCUMENTS

- In addition to choosing your business structure, you need to file the formation documents. Services like LegalZoom and legal and accounting advisors can help you with this.
- For LLCs, file Articles of Organization with your state's business registration office.
- For corporations, file Articles of Incorporation and draft corporate bylaws.
- For partnerships, draft and sign a partnership agreement.

CREATE AN OPERATING AGREEMENT OR BYLAWS

- Draft an operating agreement for LLCs or bylaws for corporations to outline the management and operational structure of the business. I used a law firm to do this for my LLC, and it cost a few thousand dollars.
- These documents provide all the details on ownership, decision-making processes, and dispute resolution. DO NOT SKIP THIS STEP because if you do not have an agreement in place and a conflict arises, you will likely have to default to the rules and regulations of the state your business is in, which can potentially put you in a disadvantageous situation.

OBTAIN BUSINESS INSURANCE

- Work with advisors to determine the types of insurance your business will need, such as general liability, professional liability, workers' compensation, and health insurance if you have employees.
- Consult with your advisors, but in general, many of these types of insurance are required by law, and you will have no choice. Additionally, depending on what kind of business you have, customers may require certain insurance levels to do business with you. This was the case for my company.

- Business insurance will be one of the most significant upfront expenses you will have to pony up before money starts coming in. But there is nothing you can do about it and having appropriate levels of insurance will help you sleep at night, so just bare with it. On the cost side, as I was dealing with a limited budget, I worked with my team of advisors to determine the bare minimum amount of insurance I could get away with initially. As time went on and our business grew, so did our insurance requirements, needs, and, unfortunately, costs.
- Purchase appropriate insurance coverage to protect your business from potential risks and monitor it annually based on the company's changing needs.

COMPLY WITH EMPLOYMENT LAWS

- Navigating and complying with employment laws can be challenging for any new business.
- Work with advisors and familiarize yourself with federal employment laws such as the Fair Labor Standards Act (FLSA), the Occupational Safety and Health Act (OSHA), the Family and Medical Leave Act (FMLA), and the Americans with Disabilities Act (ADA).
- Additionally, each state and locality may have other employment laws that must be followed. These can include minimum wage laws, workers' compensation regulations, and anti-discrimination laws.
- I highly recommend consulting with an employment law attorney to educate them about your business and get advice on how best to meet these regulations. I hired one through LegalZoom's attorney service, and it was well worth the cost of the hour or so I spent on the phone with them.
- Understand and comply with federal and state employment laws, including wage and hour laws, anti-discrimination laws, and workplace safety regulations.

- Post any required labor law posters in the workplace if you have one.

MAINTAIN ACCURATE RECORDS AND BOOKS

- We will discuss this in more detail in the Accounting chapter, but you need to maintain accurate books and records right from the get-go.
- Set up an accounting system to track income, expenses, and other financial transactions.
- Maintain accurate and up-to-date financial records for tax and regulatory purposes.
- Consider hiring a bookkeeper or accountant to assist with financial management.

FILE ANNUAL REPORTS AND RENEWALS

- File annual reports with your state's business registration office, if required.
- Renew all business licenses, permits, and registrations as needed.
- Stay informed about ongoing compliance requirements and deadlines.
- Many companies and services can do this for you for a fee. In the beginning, as I was having a hard time keeping track of them all and staying on top of them, that is what I did. Later, when I brought on an assistant, she kept track of them and did all the filings. Either way, stay on top of these because if you don't, rest assured, you WILL be paying penalties when you discover them.

INTELLECTUAL PROPERTY PROTECTION

- While this is not a law or legal requirement *per se*, you should strongly consider protecting your business's intellectual property through trademarks, copyrights, and patents. We will discuss this in more detail in a later chapter.

DATA PROTECTION AND PRIVACY COMPLIANCE

- If your company will house customer data in your environment, you must comply with data protection measures to ensure this customer and business data remains secure. If you do not, you can face severe fines and penalties.
- If applicable, ensure you comply with data privacy regulations for customer and employee data for regulations, such as the General Data Protection Regulation (GDPR) and the California Consumer Privacy Act (CCPA).
- ZZZZZZZZ…Oh sorry I fell asleep on my keyboard.

As always, consult with a legal advisor to understand your specific business requirements.

ENVIRONMENTAL REGULATIONS

- Determine if your business must comply with environmental regulations and obtain necessary permits.
- Implement practices to minimize environmental impact and ensure compliance with local, state, and federal environmental laws.

PREPARE FOR TAXES

The only difference between a tax man and a taxidermist is that the taxidermist leaves the skin.

MARK TWAIN

Oh boy, taxes—my favorite topic. Do not, and I repeat, do not mess around with taxes or the taxman.

- Keep detailed records of all financial transactions.
- You should have a strong understanding of your tax obligations, including income tax, employment, and, in particular, sales taxes.

While although there are no federal state taxes in the United States, state and local sales taxes are a super special form of a pain in the ass and something that will feel like a full-time job if you are selling nationwide as we were. As a primer, most states have different sales tax rates and categories of what you sell, being taxable or not. Additionally, different counties can even have various rules and rates in the same state. But the good news is it's entirely on you to figure this all out!

Further, in what has to be the biggest racket in the history of the universe, if you are selling products or services that are taxable in the state or county you are selling into, you also get the privilege of collecting these taxes from the customer and submitting these monies back to the government in a timely manner.

As a bonus, if you don't get these payments in right on time, even one day late in some instances, you will get the pleasure of heavy penalties. We had the pleasure of learning that even if the delay of payment happened due to the government's side of posting the transaction and government holidays delaying transactions, it would still result in you getting penalized through the nose! For us, not having our house in order in the beginning resulted in thousands and thousands of dollars in penalties.

But you at least get the added benefit of doing ALL of these collection and remittance activities with absolutely zero financial or other interest to your business! Does that sound like a good deal? It isn't! (You masochist, you.)

Can you imagine someone proposing this deal to you? It would go a little like this, and I prefer to imagine this conversation in the voice of a gangster (think Joe Pesci in *Goodfellas*) in a hushed tone in a dark alley. A complete stranger approaches you and says, "Hey, listen here, guy. I have a great deal for you. I need you to go to this address and collect some money this guy owes me. And you better get him to pay. *Kapeesh?* Then, I need you to run back over here and give me my money lickety-split." Inquisitively, you ask, "You must be nuts. What's in it for me?" He replies, "Nothing." You continue, "But why would I do this?" He replies, "Cause I told you so." You continue, "And what if I don't?" He replies, "I break your fucking legs." This is the deal you are agreeing to in collecting sales taxes on behalf of the government; congrats!

I clearly remember my conversation with my outside accountant, my buddy Brian Eagan, when he first educated me about all of this. I said to him, "You have got to be fucking kidding me, right? There is no way I have to collect all of this for free and get penalized if it's not on our time or the customer doesn't pay us on time. What the hell is in it for us?" He looked at me seriously and said, "Yes, I am serious, and there is absolutely nothing in it for you." It was a profound WTF moment. As the kids these days say, "FML." MAKE. THE. PAIN. STOP.

Now that you know all about this sales tax fun, be sure to have a rigorous process and a dedicated person to make sure the payments are submitted on time. Don't forget that some government entities want to get paid monthly and some quarterly, and you get the added benefit of tracking and understanding all of this as well. In Bill Murray's *Caddyshack* voice, "So you also have that going for you, which is nice."

- File quarterly estimated business income tax payments (if required). And if you don't pay on time, you will pay penalties. AGAIN.
- If you will have employees off the get-go, set up your payroll system or hire your outside accounting firm to handle automatically submitting payroll taxes, those fun taxes you get to pay (just shy of seven percent) on top of salaries for the pleasure of employing people and creating jobs. Thanks, Government!
- Work with a tax professional to ensure accurate and timely annual tax filings.

But at least I am not bitter about taxes, right? Okay, fine. I will leave you alone and keep working with my therapist on it. As I used to tell my employees, and you will learn more about this in the company culture section, it's fine to complain as long as you follow up with a suggestion. What are my suggestions here? I put some in the appendix if you care. You probably don't care, but I did it anyway. So there!

In conclusion, work with your advisors to determine what licenses and permits you need. Additionally, be aware of all the various taxes and have a system and team to ensure they are processed in time. Hopefully, this system of collecting and remitting taxes will be much more efficient in the future, but in the meantime, it is what it is. While these parts of running a business are not fun and can be painful, it's just part of the game. You won't ever be happy about it but know everyone else running a business will be just as pissed about it as you will be. And misery loves company. Party.

CHAPTER 9
BUSINESS FINANCES AND ACCOUNTING 101

Accounting and bookkeeping are mission-critical practices for any new business, as they involve systematically recording, organizing, and managing your business's financial transactions. You must pay great attention and take diligent care in this area of your business. Effective accounting and bookkeeping ensure accurate financial records and compliance with tax laws and provide critical information for decision-making and strategic planning, ultimately supporting your business's financial health and growth.

This is the one area of the business I was most intimidated by initially. Before I started the company, I had zero experience or exposure to accounting principles or practices, and I had never done bookkeeping. Sure, I had been responsible for managing my family's finances, but doing it on a business scale was overwhelming. Additionally, I did not have it in my budget to hire a full-time accountant in the beginning. So I did what I always did: I read. After starting the company, the first five books I read were all accounting books. For all other business areas, I figured common sense would prevail or I had experience. But for accounting, I wasn't going to mess around. If you are like me and don't have experience in this area, while initially intimidating, I am here to tell you that you will figure it out. Let's look at some of the best practices I learned and walk through the steps to ensure you and your business succeed in this area.

First, let's get some vocabulary out of the way.

Bookkeeping focuses on the day-to-day recording of transactions, such as sales, purchases, receipts, and payments, using tools like ledgers and accounting software. It is as simple as ensuring that all financial activities (i.e., money coming in and going out) are recorded. This can be simplified to be thought of as data entry activities.

Accounting, on the other hand, involves interpreting, classifying, analyzing, reporting, and summarizing financial data, providing insights through financial statements like balance sheets, income statements, and cash flow statements.

Now, let's look at what steps you need to take to get started.

SETTING UP A BUSINESS BANK ACCOUNT

Establishing a business bank account will mark your first step in structuring your company's financials. This move separates your personal assets from your company's assets. The procedure for opening a business account is pretty easy, but it typically requires a collection of legal documents, including incorporation papers, an EIN, and potentially your ownership agreements.

So, you must have gone through the incorporation process, created the basic business agreements, and then provided them to the bank. Don't think you have to be some huge business to start a business account. It's simply not the case. Most business checking accounts are free and don't require a large upfront deposit.

When thinking through what bank to use, consider what level of personal touch you desire and if you will go for a line of credit right from the get-go. This will help your decision-making process. If you don't think you will go out for a line of credit (which, frankly, will be hard to do for brand-new companies since there is no financial history), this opens you up to a litany of options, and you can even default to where you do your personal checking. That is what I do for my current businesses. I use Chase, and I like seeing all my personal and business bank accounts on one dashboard.

But for Controle, we initially used Bank of America. Years later, we moved to a regional bank because I wanted a more personal touch and local feel and wanted to establish a line of credit. As an FYI, once you go for a line of credit, the bank that gives it to you will likely force you to do the rest of your banking with them.

But besides that, consider whether a large bank with basically zero contact will be ok with you or if you want to go with a smaller bank that might have fewer bells and whistles but will provide more of that local feel and touch. Either way, setting up the account will take an hour or so. As of writing this, I have had to go into a branch every time I have had to establish a business checking account for the various companies I own today. However, things might have changed by the time you have read this to allow for opening one online.

SETTING UP AN ACCOUNTING SYSTEM

Once you establish the bank account, focus on how you will do bookkeeping. Choosing and setting up an accounting software system right at the beginning of the company is a good practice. The selection of accounting software represents an important decision. It is a choice that not only can provide bookkeeping but, down the line, can streamline operations and enhance efficiency. There are many options, each with unique features, from basic expense tracking to complex financial forecasting. The criteria for selection should be based on your business's specific needs, size, and growth trajectory.

For brand-new businesses, I recommend simplicity and user-friendliness, ensuring that financial management is not overbearing for you in the beginning. Another option, which is what I did, is to interview accounting firms right from the start and ask what tools they recommend. You will want to use the tool favored by the company helping you. Almost all suggested using QuickBooks—either the desktop version or the online version at quickbooks.com. Quickbooks has been around for a long time in the accounting world, and I found that almost everyone was familiar with it.

Ultimately, I greatly favored SaaS offerings, so I didn't have to deal with installing and updating hardware-based software products. Ultimately, I chose QuickBooks.com and continue to use it for all of my businesses. It provides everything you need for a low $35 per month cost, is simple to use, and provides easy access for outside companies to log in remotely and help you out. It also offers advanced capabilities like payroll and credit card processing for an additional cost as the needs of the business increase. But it is certainly not the only option out there; there are many others you can explore.

SELECT AN OUTSIDE ACCOUNTING FIRM TO HELP

One thing you will want to strongly consider, and ultimately, this is the route I chose, is to hire an outside accounting firm to help you right out of the get-go. At the beginning of the business, everything is so new and scary, and it will seem like things are happening a million miles per hour. One critical aspect that can significantly impact your success is the financial management of the business.

Outside accounting firms have all "been there, done that" and can help you set up your financial infrastructure and avoid typical pitfalls. Many of them offer a variety of services tailored to you and based on your budget and needs. Ultimately, I chose to hire an accounting firm on an hourly basis. In my first meeting with them, I told them I wanted them to walk me through everything they felt a new business needed to do and how to do basic bookkeeping. They offered bookkeeping services for organizations, but since my business had only a small number of large invoices and QuickBooks could automatically connect to my business checking account, where I managed all expenses, it was simple for me to handle the bookkeeping at the beginning. Then, I had them on speed dial whenever I ran into issues with the software and had questions. It worked and didn't cost me over $500 to $2,000 per quarter. It was well worth the money.

As we grew and our needs became more complicated, I had my assistant, Chrissy, who had some bookkeeping experience, take this on. We continued to contract with the outside accounting firm, and they became an instrumental part of our success. My assistant worked with their team daily to ensure the transactions were accurately recorded and for tax obligations. And I worked with what essentially became our outsourced Chief Financial Officer (CFO) for more strategic conversations and advanced financial decisions. This worked like a charm for me. This essential outsourced CFO, my buddy Brian Eagan at a company named Selden Fox, became a valuable member of the company and whom I used extensively and strategically when selling the company. Business success primarily comes down to the team you build around you, and having an outside firm specializing in accounting is a valuable member to add to the team.

UNDERSTANDING FINANCIAL STATEMENTS

After you select the accounting system or firm, you will need to get a basic understanding of financial statements—the balance sheet, income statement, and cash flow statement—as they paint the picture of your business's financial performance and are critical to understand. Let's look at the differences and purposes of these reports now.

Balance Sheet

The balance sheet is the financial statement that provides a snapshot of your company's financial position at a specific point in time. It summarizes your company's assets, liabilities, and shareholders' equity, offering insights into what the company owns and owes and the amount invested by shareholders.

Examples of assets are how much cash you have in the bank, accounts receivable (what invoices you have out to customers but are still waiting on payment), inventory (if applicable) that is already purchased and ready to be sold, and short-term investments. An example of a "short-term investment" would be if you had extra cash saved up and invested in savings accounts, money market funds, and certificates of deposit (CDs) as an example. A short-term investment should be low-risk and highly liquid to be considered part of the balance sheet.

Liabilities are things you owe someone money on. These can be accounts payable items (what invoices people have out to you but still need to pay for), any short-term loans you have taken out (if applicable), and accrued expenses. An accrued expense is a term that essentially means something that you will owe money on because you have used it. However, you have yet to receive an invoice, or you still need to record it. A common one is salaries and wages for your employees. Since most companies pay two weeks in arrears, you eventually owe your employee for the time over those two weeks but just have yet to pay them. That is an accrued expense.

Shareholders' equity, also known as stockholders' equity or owners' equity, is more confusing. It represents the balance of a company's assets after deducting liabilities. It reflects the company's net worth, not necessarily from what you could sell it for, but instead from the perspective of its shareholders and shows the shareholders' ownership interest in the company. A strong shareholders' equity position generally indicates a healthy financial status, implying that the company has sufficient assets to cover its liabilities and still provides value to its shareholders.

In summary, the balance sheet is a snapshot at a point in time that reveals the company's assets, liabilities, and equity, reflecting its stability and liquidity. This is one of the reports that all banks, creditors, and investors will want to look at to gauge the business's overall financial health.

Income Statement

The income statement, or profit and loss statement (or P&L statement for short), is the financial document that summarizes your company's revenues, expenses, and profits or losses over a specific period, typically a fiscal quarter or year. It provides a detailed account of how your company's operations have performed financially, showing whether the company made a profit or incurred a loss during the period. This is essentially the "money coming in, money going out" snapshot report. As a business owner, it will be the financial report you look at most frequently, or at least it was for me.

The P&L statement provides a solid basis for tracking profitability quarter over quarter and is a key report to help you decide whether to put your foot on the gas or scale back a bit. When running a business, especially in the beginning, it is tempting and easy to go off of your "gut feel" of how the company is performing. I am not suggesting that paying attention to your gut isn't important because it is, but you must back it up with raw data and analytics. The P&L report will be your main aid in determining the business's financial health.

Cash Flow Statement

Lastly, the cash flow statement is the financial document that provides a detailed summary of your business's cash inflows and outflows over a specific period, typically a fiscal quarter or year.

The cash flow statement shows how changes in the balance sheet and income statement affect cash and cash equivalents. It provides insight into your company's ability to generate cash (selling stuff) to meet short-term obligations (payroll and payments to suppliers) and fund its operations (all the other stuff like travel, software subscriptions, etc.).

Many people think companies fail because they are not selling enough of whatever they sell. But that is not typically the case. The primary reason many companies fail is that they run out of cash. It could be poor cash management or unfortunate timing when receiving cash from suppliers, but either way, as the old adage goes, "cash is king." Understanding the cash flow statement and keeping an eye on it is crucial to understand your risk of running out of cash and getting ahead of it before it happens.

Together, these documents provide a comprehensive view of your company's financial status and will aid you in strategic decision-making and investment considerations. Although some terms and concepts associated with these reports might still confuse you, it's ok. Eventually, you will understand them and how to use them to your advantage. At the end of the day, this is not rocket science. Your role is to understand their output and use them as compasses for where the company is and where to take it.

As mentioned, it's totally ok if you don't have an accounting degree when starting a business. You will figure it out. If you feel, like I did, still a bit unconfident in this area, there are plenty of books to read and other resources to get you up to speed. Accounting is more science than art and is relatively black and white. And who knows, you may even come to like it. I was proud of myself at the end of the journey of Controle of my ability to understand accounting principles and terms, especially since I started from zero. Genuinely understanding accounting principles will become a valuable asset for you, especially if and when you look to sell the company.

PHASE FOUR
LAUNCH PHASE—YOU AND MINDSET

Now that we have laid the foundation of your business, you need to recognize that the key to its success lies in one person's hands, and that's YOU, girlfriend! In this phase, we'll cover how to shift your mindset from employee to entrepreneur, develop new skills for tackling challenges, and address the emotional toll a business can take—and how to manage it. Throughout the chapters, I'll share tactics and habits for overcoming these obstacles. I wanted to dive deep into these topics, and I did not shortchange you. Many of the business books out there gloss over these topics or don't discuss them at all. That's a huge miss. Don't skip these chapters.

CHAPTER 10
FROM EMPLOYEE TO ENTREPRENEUR - THE PSYCHOLOGICAL BLUEPRINT

> *Starting your own business isn't just a job—it's a way of life.*
>
> REID HOFFMAN, CO-FOUNDER OF LINKEDIN

When you leave the Corporate World behind and take on the life of an entrepreneur, you must unlearn many of your old habits and cultivate new ones. The beginning of this transformation is adopting an entrepreneurial mindset, which will change how you view challenges, risks, and uncertainties. Unlike the structured environment you are used to as an employee, where you know what to expect day in and day out, entrepreneurship is filled with fluidity and ambiguity. Navigating this new landscape requires mental agility that is learned and earned through experience. But make no mistake, every successful entrepreneur has developed and cultivated these new skills. Below, I will walk you through some of the tools and tactics I have employed to help you on your journey.

THE RISK-REWARD DILEMMA

 The biggest risk is not taking any risk. In a world that's changing really quickly, the only strategy that is guaranteed to fail is not taking risks.

MARK ZUCKERBERG

The first psychological shift involves embracing risk as an integral component of growth. As the saying goes, "No risk, no reward." When it comes to employment, risk is often perceived as a threat to stability and security. Therefore, you may already be programmed to inherently think of risk as a bad thing.

In the first six months of starting my business, I heard the word risk more times in those six months than I had in the previous 30-plus years on the planet. I constantly heard, "Yeah, I thought about starting my own business too, but I figured there was too much risk." What risk? Fuck off. Clearly, these people didn't do the fear-setting exercise. They let the fear control them and not the other way around. That's a big difference between people who make the leap and those who "thought about it" but never did anything and spend the rest of their lives thinking, *What if?* Don't be a "what-if" person.

There will always be an element of risk in running a business, but you can and will learn how to mitigate it. And remember, you can't have rewards without risk. When you have your own business, the rewards can be MASSIVE. They are so potentially massive that you can dramatically change your life, and your actions can change multiple generations of your family's lives, as they have for me. These risks are the gateway you must pass to fulfill all your wildest dreams. Can risks be scary? Sure. But as George Addair said, "Everything you have ever wanted is on the other side of fear." So stare that fear right in the face and say, "Not today, Satan."

For entrepreneurs, risk is the lens you must constantly look through, and it is where innovation and breakthroughs emerge. This reorientation toward risk doesn't mean you should start acting recklessly;

instead, you will need to develop the ability to assess and find opportunities where others see insurmountable challenges. It's about learning to weigh the potential benefits against the downside and then making informed decisions to propel the business forward.

Whenever I weighed making a big decision, I did a simple risk-reward exercise. It does not need to be more complicated than looking at the downside of a decision versus the upside. If the downside is much more than the upside, it's an obvious choice; you reject it and move on. If the downside is close to the upside, I will probably not do it as there are competing activities for my time, and I want to invest my time in significant upside items. Finally, if the upside is much more than the downside, I would go for it and not think of it again. Doing a pros and cons list is also helpful for any of the decisions you are on the fence about. At the end of the day, you can use as much information as you have, but as an entrepreneur, you will constantly need to make decisions with little or incomplete information.

If, after going through this process, you are still stuck on which way to go on a decision, always go with your gut. You will be the one who must live with the decision, and if you go with your gut, even if others disagree, you can sleep at night. Does that mean you will always make the right decision? Absolutely not. But you will be able to live with it regardless of the outcome. Looking back at some of my worst decisions, in most cases, they were ones where I went against my gut.

THE MINDSET OF TAKING ACTION AND DECISION-MAKING

Whenever you see a successful business, someone once made a courageous decision.

PETER DRUCKER, MANAGEMENT CONSULTANT

Another critical shift in being an entrepreneur is moving from a mindset of seeking permission to taking initiative. Employees are accustomed to operating within the confines of their job descriptions, often requiring approval before taking action. "Is it ok if I go to the bathroom, boss?" Entrepreneurs, on the other hand, thrive on autonomy, making decisions swiftly and independently. This transition can be exhilarating yet daunting, requiring a recalibration of your comfort with making decisions in the face of incomplete information. It's about cultivating confidence in your judgment and learning to trust the process, even when the outcome is uncertain.

This new paradigm of making decisions swiftly does not mean you have to be hasty. Many times, when I was on the fence about an important decision and people were pressing me for an answer, I told them I had to sleep on it. Do not allow others to pressure you into making big or important decisions. I promise you they will certainly try, especially when they have something to gain from you not thinking it through. You must get accustomed to making decisions quickly, but that does not mean they have to be made immediately. You will want the time to process it, perform your risk-reward calculation, talk to your gut, decide, and move on.

DEALING WITH UNCERTAINTY AND INSTABILITY

Dealing with uncertainty will become a daily endeavor for you. Unlike the predictable rhythm of a nine-to-five job, where your day-to-day doesn't change much, entrepreneurship is stepping out into the unknown every day. Managing this uncertainty will require stoic resilience, an ability to remain steadfast in pursuing your vision, even when the path is fraught with obstacles and naysayers.

There are many strategies for coping with this instability. The first includes setting short-term, achievable goals that provide a sense of progress and direction. Initially, set goals based on the variables you control, e.g., completing the website, securing a domain name, and reaching out to three potential partners about partnering.

Another strategy for dealing with instability is celebrating victories, even small ones. The shift to owning a business is different in the beginning because most successes happen in the dark. Unless you are starting the company with others, you will be the only one who understands the victory. You will have to become your own cheerleader.

Additionally, if you have a spouse, share your victories with them, no matter how small. My wife did a tremendous job of this for me in the beginning: "Oh wow, that's great, hun," even though she had no clue what I was talking about. If it is not your spouse, find a friend or someone you can share with. This could even be a therapist if you have one. If you don't, I highly recommend getting one to help with the ups and downs of entrepreneurship. (I will talk more about this later on in this section.) Celebrating these small victories will help keep some sense of normalcy and motivate you to keep going until things become more stable.

THE NINETY-DAY PLAN

Another tactic for dealing with the instability of starting a business involves initially only looking ninety days out. There are a lot of books and "experts" that will say you need to be thinking long term—years out—in the beginning. That's a crock of shit. Initially, you just want to worry about the next ninety days and how to keep the money flowing in. You can learn to strategize about longer-term goals like selling the company, which we will get into later, as you get bigger and have help. But for now, look at ninety days out. Anything much further than that will produce anxiety because, in the beginning, you literally don't know how it is going to go, so why project what could happen? It's an effective use of your time to look ninety days out, as that is a more realistic gauge of what you can predict or guesstimate.

CULTIVATING A POSITIVE MINDSET

Gratitude is not only the greatest of virtues but the parent of all the others.

MARCUS TULLIUS CICERO, ROMAN PHILOSOPHER

Another tactic for shifting from an employee to an entrepreneur is developing a positive mindset. I get it—it is much easier to be a miserable prick and focus on the negatives in life or business. Yes, life is hard, and shit happens all the time. And in business, the vast majority of the time, you are being told no, or roadblocks are getting in your way. None of it is fair and will never be, so just get over it already.

The first step in cultivating a positive mindset is developing an attitude of gratitude. As mentioned, life and running a business are hard, but guess what? They're also incredible. It comes down to what you focus on, and it is virtually impossible to be mad when you think about what you are grateful for.

One helpful daily exercise I learned from Scott Adams, creator of Dilbert, in his book *How to Fail at Almost Everything and Still Win Big*, is keeping a gratitude journal to help develop a positive attitude. I have a gratitude journal that I have written in every day for years. Every morning, when I first get to my computer, I write five things I am grateful for (things that happened or are happening), five affirmations (things I want for the future) that I also learned from Scott's book, and general thoughts about what's making me anxious. Now, this doesn't mean I am always thrilled about the exercise or in a positive mood before I do it. Somedays, I wake up in a shitty mood or have just dealt with something annoying before I sit down, and I don't feel like doing it. But I still proceed, and I find it helps. Just like working out at the gym, it's not something you are always thrilled about doing, but you always feel better in the end. Your brain is a muscle that needs working out like your body.

Another exercise to use to develop a positive attitude is forcing yourself to look at setbacks as opportunities. Years into the business, I heard Tim Ferris interview Jocko Willink, a badass of a human being who is a retired Navy Seal officer and motivational speaker. I was blown away by Jockos' perspective on adversity and using it to develop a positive mindset, and I started using it in my daily life. In this podcast, Jocko spoke about his "good" philosophy, which is his take on how to deal with adversity. Let's hear directly from him: "When things are going bad, there's going to be some good that will come from it. Oh, the mission got canceled? Good. We can focus on another one." "Didn't get promoted? Good. More time to get better." Didn't get funded? Good. We own more of the company." "Unexpected problems? Good. We have the opportunity to figure out a solution." So when you inevitably are faced with what appears to be a shitty position, ask yourself what the good is in this situation.

In conclusion, as an entrepreneur, you will face challenges and opportunities that most others in the Corporate World simply do not face. This is not something to run from but instead, run towards. By developing and cultivating an entrepreneurial mindset you will be primed and ready for whatever comes your way.

CHAPTER 11
PUNCHING BACK— DEVELOPING RESILIENCE PRACTICES

> *Everyone has a plan until they get punched in the mouth.*
>
> MIKE TYSON, BRILLIANT PHILOSOPHER AND WORLD HEAVYWEIGHT BOXING CHAMPION

In business, it's not a matter of IF you will get punched in the mouth; it's about how often and how hard it will be. Plan on it. Every single entrepreneur's success story has obstacles as a major part of it. It's not about succeeding in the absence of obstacles; it's about learning to push through them and getting to the final bell. Let's look at some examples of entrepreneurs who pushed through obstacles and achieved great success:

Walt Disney had multiple business failures, including the bankruptcy of his first animation studio and the loss of his character, Oswald the Lucky Rabbit, to his distributor. I am sure this made Walt feel like an unlucky rabbit and would make many stop, but he didn't. Disney bounced back, created Mickey Mouse, and continued innovating in the animation industry. And we all know what happened next: The Walt Disney Company has grown into one of the world's largest and most influential entertainment companies. Disney movies and entertainment were a massive influence in my childhood, and they most likely were for you as well. Imagine if he would have stopped at that first face of adversity.

J.K. Rowling, author of the Harry Potter series, faced numerous challenges on her path to having one of the best-selling books in history. She faced numerous rejections from publishers, faced severe financial difficulties, and dealt with depression. Even though her manuscripts were initially balked at, she continued working on them in cafes, often bringing her daughter along because she could not afford heating in her apartment. Despite these challenges, she persevered, believed in herself, and continued writing. When her first book was finally published in 1997, it became a massive success, led to one of the most beloved book series ever, and made her one of the most well-known and wealthiest authors.

These stories underscore a common theme: resilience in the face of adversity is about evolving from it. Whether refining a business model based on feedback or pivoting to new strategies in response to unforeseen challenges, you must learn how to overcome these obstacles.

So, how do we learn how to overcome the inevitable setbacks? I am glad you asked! Wow, you really are smart. It's like you read my mind. Put on your boxing gloves because we must now step into the gym and learn about the counterpunch: resilience. Resilience is the capacity to recover quickly from difficulties. Developing resilience practices, those skills that will help you recover swiftly and allow you to punch back is a skill you must learn to adapt. Building resilience is like muscle strengthening; it requires consistent effort and the proper practices. Buckle up, Buttercup, and step into the ring. For this next chapter, I am your Cus D'Amato.

EXERCISE 1: MEDITATION

 Transcendental Meditation gives me an island of calm in the midst of so much turbulence.

PAUL MCCARTNEY

One effective technique for developing resilience is mindfulness meditation, which has been shown to reduce stress and anxiety and enhance emotional stability. With meditation, you can take that punch, deeply absorb it, and return with renewed energy, throwing haymakers. Meditation has been a massive part of my success. About two years after starting the company, I felt like I needed additional tools to manage the day-to-day stresses of running the company. I had heard many celebrities that I followed and admired (Howard Stern, Jerry Seinfeld, Paul McCartney, and Oprah Winfrey, to name a few) talk about a particular type of meditation, Transcendental Meditation (tm.org), and how it was a major part of their life and success. I decided to get trained on it, and I can tell you there has been no better investment I have ever made in myself than learning TM. TM is practiced by sitting comfortably with closed eyes for about twenty minutes twice daily. The core of TM is using a mantra: a specific sound, word, or phrase that is silently repeated to facilitate deep relaxation and promote peaceful awareness. It is both simple in its practice and powerful in results.

Here I am almost ten years later, and I continue to practice it every day, twice a day, for twenty minutes. The benefits of meditation are MASSIVE. I am much calmer; I do not overreact like I used to, and I have much greater mental clarity. Overall, TM has made me a better person, and I do everything better in my life because of it. Further, meditation opens creative portals that are only accessible through its practice. As a result, many of my best business ideas (including ones for this book) and conflict resolution solutions popped into my head during my TM sessions.

Meditation also teaches you how to deal with and process adversity in a healthy way. When I was running the company and the shit was hitting the fan, I had many times when my teammates would say, "Wow, you seem to be handling this well." Additionally, I would get compliments on my ability to compartmentalize issues or, in other words, not let one situation affect all other situations. This was one hundred percent my practice of TM on display.

Additionally, about a year before writing this book, I got a neurofeedback brain map (a fascinating area of neuroscience) to identify potential areas that could help strengthen my mental fortitude. My brain map came back exceedingly positive. The doctor told me that I was not a candidate for their services. I asked him how often that happened, and he said not often at all. Then he said something that stuck with me. "This is clearly the result of a heavily meditated brain." I am not saying all of this to brag—it doesn't say anything about me, but it does say a whole lot about meditation.

Getting certified comes at a cost, but TM is not the only available option. There are many apps available around meditation (Calm and Headspace, for example) that are affordable, and others find effective. It is less about the form of meditation and more about the practice of meditation. I cannot encourage you enough to do it. It's a superpower and game-changer. If you don't meditate, I will do most everything better than you because I meditate, and you don't. Yeah, I said it.

EXERCISE 2: PHYSICAL ACTIVITY

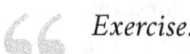 *Exercise.*

> RICHARD BRANSON'S RESPONSE ABOUT HIS TOP
> TIP FOR SUCCESS

Another practice is setting aside time for physical activity, which improves physical health and boosts mental well-being, making one better equipped to handle the stresses of entrepreneurship. For me, I have to work out at least every other day. If I don't, I feel lethargic and not at my best. In particular, the activity I do the most is running. I don't even like the process of running, but I love how it makes me feel. And you don't have to be a marathoner to get the "runners high" benefits. I usually only run for one to two miles. I pop in my AirPods, run at about seventy-five percent of my max, and am done in fifteen to twenty minutes. For the rest of the day, I feel fantastic.

There are many different physical activities, and studies have shown that physically active people are much healthier and happier. If you are reading this and don't do a lot of physical activity, start. It pays massive dividends in life and your business success. Whenever I was particularly stressed or felt burnt out, I ran, and everything seemed easier to deal with. On the flip side, when I was overly excited about something that had happened (which is a great thing) and felt like I couldn't calm down, I would also go for a run and always breathe easier. Further, when I felt sick or down, I would go for a run and immediately feel better. It's a magic cure-all.

EXERCISE 3: VITAMINS

> *I've seen the profound impact that smart supplementation can have on myself and thousands of readers. It can be the difference between feeling like crap and feeling like Superman.*
>
> TIM FERRISS, ENTREPRENEUR AND NEW YORK TIMES BEST-SELLING AUTHOR

Vitamins, those essential micronutrients that the body requires for a range of biochemical functions, hold a special place in the entrepreneurial toolkit. They support various bodily functions that can directly and indirectly impact your performance, resilience, and overall health. Now, I am certainly not a doctor, so don't take any of this as medical advice. Obviously, please consult with your doctor or healthcare professional, but I found the following vitamins helpful.

Vitamin B and, specifically, a B-complex (including B6, B12, and folate) play a crucial role in energy production and the proper functioning of the brain, enhancing cognitive abilities such as memory, concentration, and decision-making. I take a vitamin B-complex every day to this day, and it is the one vitamin that makes my whole day feel different when I do not take it. This is my absolute go-to and one I do not miss.

Vitamins A, C, D, and E, on the other hand, contribute to the immune system's strength. Entrepreneurs often work long hours and frequently experience significant stress, so our immune response system can get compromised. Regular intake of these vitamins can help fortify your body's defenses against common illnesses. Further, vitamin D has been linked to mood regulation, and A, C, and E can help combat oxidative stress and inflammation, conditions often exacerbated by stress.

A simple multivitamin can help provide these, and many are available online or at health food stores for purchase. One supplement that I take, as introduced to me by Tim Ferriss in *The Four-Hour Body*, is Athletic Greens, also known as AG1. It's a powder form that can be added to a drink and essentially serves as a multivitamin. I noticed a significant difference in how I felt when I first started taking it, and I still take it to this day.

Vitamins ensure you can perform at your best by enhancing brain function, boosting the immune system, improving mood, and combating stress. As mentioned, work with your doctor or healthcare professional to determine a plan for you in this area. Don't skip this step. The better your body and brain function, the better you will perform, and your business will follow suit.

EXERCISE 4: SLEEP

Sleep is a performance enhancer. If you prioritize it, it can lead to better health, less stress, and more joy.

ARIANNA HUFFINGTON, AUTHOR AND CO-FOUNDER OF THE HUFFINGTON POST

Ahh, one of my favorite topics: sleep! I consider myself a sleep nerd. Just ask any of my friends or my wife: I can be annoying by how much I talk about sleep, its importance, and the different hacks that I have come up with to increase my quality and quantity of sleep. And after I went to edit the first draft of this section, I thought to myself, *Holy shit, this section is WAY TOO LONG.* So, for this final version of the book, I will abbreviate it, as I didn't want to lull you to sleep. HEY OH! *Oh girl, please tell me he isn't going to start making jokes again.*

But for you, and only you, since we are now besties (don't tell the other readers, ok?), if you give this book an online review and send me proof to review@itstheblueprint.com, as a bonus, I will provide this bonus chapter to you with all my added sleep info and hacks I have come up with for free. #Winning! But in all seriousness, I would really appreciate it. I will provide not only the bonus chapter on sleep and sleep hacks but also some other goodies I will mention later and at the end of the book.

Okay, Jesus, Kevin, enough groveling. Leave these poor people alone. Let's get back to our regularly scheduled program. Okay, sorry. Back to sleep.

Ever since I was a newborn, I have been sleep-sensitive. My mom told me I slept way more than my siblings and that trend of needing sleep to perform at my best has continued throughout my life. On any given day, my mood and how I feel are directly correlated to the quantity and quality of the sleep I get. However, this can be a real challenge for entrepreneurs, where long hours and high stress are often the norm. Before we talk about how to best combat this challenge, let's look at the importance of sleep in the role of a successful entrepreneur.

- **Benefits of Sleep:** Sleep is a basic human need that affects every aspect of our cognitive, emotional, and physical functioning. Proper sleep enhances memory, improves concentration, boosts creativity, and strengthens decision-making abilities—all crucial for navigating the complexities of starting and running a business.
- **Cognitive Enhancement:** Sleep plays an important role in mental processes. It helps consolidate memory, enabling entrepreneurs to retain and recall information effectively.
- **Emotional Resilience:** Entrepreneurship is often an emotional rollercoaster, with highs of success and lows of setbacks. Sleep helps regulate mood and manage emotional responses, ensuring you can maintain a calm demeanor in various challenging situations.
- **Physical Health:** The physical demands of long workdays require an entrepreneur's body to be in top condition. Sleep is crucial for physical recovery and maintenance.
- **Improved Decision-Making:** Lack of sleep can impair judgment and increase impulsivity. For entrepreneurs, where each decision can have significant implications, being well-rested can mean the difference between making a calculated decision and one that is hasty and poorly thought out. Wait, maybe we shouldn't have purchased that leer jet in the first six months of the business! Sleep enhances these cognitive functions related to evaluating risks and benefits.

Practical Strategies for Enhancing Sleep

Here are some well-known practices for enhancing sleep.

- **Consistency**: Adhering to a consistent sleep schedule strengthens the circadian rhythm, improving sleep quality. Adhering to this schedule will admittedly be hard for you in the early years of the business. Or you could be like me in the beginning and have a consistent schedule, but consistently not getting enough sleep.

- **Environment**: Optimizing your sleep environment, including a comfortable mattress, minimal noise, and making the room as dark as possible, can significantly enhance sleep quality. Even small lights emanating from your chargers and cable boxes can disrupt sleep. I put electrical tape on these devices that have lights on them.
- **Pre-Sleep Routine**: Engaging in a relaxing pre-sleep routine, such as reading or meditation, can help signal to the body that it's time to wind down. Watching 30 minutes of ESPN Sports Center helped me unwind and signaled to my body that it was time to sleep.
- **Technology Detox**: Limiting screen time before bed can mitigate the effects of blue light, which can disrupt the natural sleep cycle. Admittedly, it's also hard to do, but studies show it does help.
- **Naps**: Strategic napping can help mitigate not getting enough sleep. I know a number of entrepreneurs who have a couch in their office and take 30-minute naps while at work during the day. If I was ever really stressed out and had headaches as a result, a 30-minute post-work nap did wonders.

I have tested dozens of products and techniques to help aid me in my sleep. In the bonus chapter after your review, I will provide the top ten tips and hacks I have developed to come up with sleep.

In summary, for entrepreneurs aiming for peak performance, integrating effective sleep practices into their lifestyle is not just beneficial—it's essential. Sleep is a powerful tool for enhancing mental acuity, emotional strength, decision-making capabilities, and overall physical health. Embracing good sleep habits can significantly amplify your ability to succeed and sustain high performance over time. Don't sleep on this tool. HEY OH! *Wow, ANOTHER sleep pun?*

Now that we have discussed the different resistance exercises, you are ready for the big fight! Just like any regime, these practices are only as effective as your ability to consistently adhere to them. Discipline is a key characteristic for the entrepreneur and one you must develop to maintain your exercises. Now that we have our bodies primed and pumped, let's get into the emotional side of the entrepreneur and the support system we must develop to help combat that side of the fight.

CHAPTER 12
UNDERSTANDING THE EMOTIONAL TOLL OF THE ENTREPRENEUR

> *As a startup CEO, I slept like a baby. I woke up every two hours and cried.*
>
> BEN HOROWITZ, CO-FOUNDER OF ANDREESSEN HOROWITZ, VENTURE CAPITALIST

Just like anything, entrepreneurship has pros and cons. The pros greatly outweigh the cons, but one of the struggles you must learn to combat is the emotional toll it can take on you. It, indeed, is an emotional roller coaster. I used to joke with people that, being an entrepreneur, some days are the best days of your life, some days are the worst days of your life, and some days both happen on the same day!

Additionally, it was almost comical how I felt on specific days of the week, and looking back, I could see the pattern. Here is what I call the daily entrepreneur mood calendar, and it mimics precisely how I felt on what day of the week it was:

DAILY ENTREPRENEUR MOOD CALENDAR

MON	TUE	WED	THU	FRI	SAT	SUN
WE ARE DOOMED	THIS IS REALLY HARD	WE ARE REALLY MAKING PROGRESS	I CAN'T BELIEVE THAT JUST HAPPENED!	WE ARE GOING TO TAKE ON THE WORLD!	I LOVE MY LIFE	I DON'T KNOW IF I CAN DO ANOTHER WEEK OF THIS
WE ARE DOOMED	THIS IS REALLY HARD	WE ARE REALLY MAKING PROGRESS	I CAN'T BELIEVE THAT JUST HAPPENED!	WE ARE GOING TO TAKE ON THE WORLD!	I LOVE MY LIFE	I DON'T KNOW IF I CAN DO ANOTHER WEEK OF THIS
WE ARE DOOMED	THIS IS REALLY HARD	WE ARE REALLY MAKING PROGRESS	I CAN'T BELIEVE THAT JUST HAPPENED!	WE ARE GOING TO TAKE ON THE WORLD!	I LOVE MY LIFE	I DON'T KNOW IF I CAN DO ANOTHER WEEK OF THIS
WE ARE DOOMED	THIS IS REALLY HARD	WE ARE REALLY MAKING PROGRESS	I CAN'T BELIEVE THAT JUST HAPPENED!	WE ARE GOING TO TAKE ON THE WORLD!	I LOVE MY LIFE	I DON'T KNOW IF I CAN DO ANOTHER WEEK OF THIS

It's comical how predictable this was for me. The key is not to fight it but to embrace it and understand that there are tools and tactics to combat it. Let's talk about tactics for navigating these psychological challenges.

THE ENTREPRENEUR SUPPORT SYSTEM

Building a robust support system is central to navigating these psychological shifts. The transition from employee to entrepreneur can be a solitary path, filled with moments of doubt and introspection. Because of this, building a network of mentors, peers, and advisors who have traversed this path or can support you is invaluable. This network provides practical advice, insights, and emotional support and can serve as a sounding board during your moments of uncertainty.

It's about creating a community for yourself that nurtures growth, offers encouragement, and provides a sense of belonging in the entrepreneurial ecosystem. These can take many forms, both inside and outside your business environment. Let's look at some now.

Mentors

One of the most valuable people in my community was my mentor, Dan, whom I could call when I got stuck. Now, you do not want to abuse having and working with a mentor. You have to use these mentor resources sparingly, as they are also swamped. Simple text messages are useful, and if I was really stuck and didn't have answers, I would ask him for ten minutes on the phone. I would take the call whenever was convenient for him (early morning, late at night).

The lessons you can learn from those who have "been there and done that" are invaluable. Those who have been doing it for a while aren't going to get tripped up by whatever you are dealing with. I would call Dan and spew for five minutes about what was going on, and then at the end, he would say, "Just do this." And he was right every single time.

I actually found it incredibly frustrating that I would spend weeks noodling on the problem, and within five minutes, he could solve it for me. I used to joke with him about it. He used the analogy that running a business was like playing a video game. The first few times, you are going to round the corner and get shot by that sniper. But next time you play, you will go slowly around that corner, know the sniper is there, and make a countermove. So, find yourself someone who has played the game before.

But what do we do if we don't have a mentor? Go back to the beginning of the folks you spoke to about starting your own business. One of them may serve as your mentor. It is less about finding someone in the same type of business as you; it's about finding someone who has experienced the mental challenges of being an entrepreneur and can support you when you're struggling.

Associations

Additionally, many associations are focused on entrepreneurs, and you can join them to meet like-minded folks. I personally did join a few of them (Young Entrepreneur Council and went through the process for Young Presidents' Organization but didn't meet the criteria), but due to how fast my company grew and my obligations on the home front, I found it challenging to make the time to invest in them. But I also had my mentor already identified.

Here are some notable organizations and platforms where entrepreneurs can connect and collaborate:

1. **Young Entrepreneur Council (YEC):** YEC is an invitation-only organization comprised of the world's most successful young entrepreneurs. Members are typically under forty-five and have founded or co-founded a business that generates substantial revenue or has secured significant funding. Here is my YEC profile along with my buddy Yottabyte, whom you will meet later on: https://businesscollective.com/kevin-barnicle-controle/index.html
2. **Young Presidents' Organization (YPO):** YPO is a global leadership community of chief executives driven by the shared belief that the world needs better leaders.
3. **Entrepreneurs' Organization (EO)**: A global network exclusively for entrepreneurs, EO offers members the opportunity to learn and grow through peer-to-peer learning, once-in-a-lifetime experiences, and connections to experts.
4. **Y Combinator (YC)**: Known for its startup accelerator, Y Combinator offers a network that continues to support entrepreneurs through funding, advice, and connections.
5. **National Association for the Self-Employed (NASE):** This organization provides day-to-day support, including benefits and resources, to help entrepreneurs and freelancers succeed.
6. **Small Business Administration (SBA):** While not a traditional networking organization, the SBA offers networking events, workshops, and mentorship opportunities through local offices and its extensive partner network.
7. **Techstars**: A global platform that offers access to capital, one-on-one mentorship, and customized programming for startup entrepreneurs.

8. **Meetup**: This is an online platform where you can find or create local groups on many topics, including entrepreneur-focused events, tech talks, and startup workshops.
9. **LinkedIn Groups**: LinkedIn hosts numerous groups for entrepreneurs where you can network, ask questions, and gain insights from other business owners across the globe.

Spouse/Friends/Family

Supporting an entrepreneur through the turbulent business journey is a pivotal role that spouses, friends, and family members can play, significantly influencing your success and well-being. One of the most essential forms of support is emotional. Being there to listen and provide reassurance during stressful times can help maintain a strong, supportive relationship. My wife used to joke with me that she was my cheerleader, and she was.

As mentioned, being an entrepreneur is an emotional rollercoaster, and don't be surprised if you get taken for the ride. Having someone there to understand this kind of bipolar existence (at least in the beginning) and to be able to support you cannot be understated. My wife did a tremendous job at this. If you let others in, you will be surprised by the great advice they will give you. I have always been open with my emotions, maybe to a fault, and am pretty transparent. Because of this openness, my wife could be an outside observer and give practical advice, especially when I was dealing with a difficult employee or human interactions. She was absolutely a part of my team.

Further, finding friends who are in similar situations can be helpful. Years later, in year seven of my business, I went through the process of selling a piece of my company. It was an intense and emotionally charged endeavor. Ever sell a house and know how stressful it is to have a home inspection on your home? Well, do that every single day for two to three months, and that is what selling your company feels like.

Fortunately, and somewhat serendipitously, I had a good friend, Justin Finnegan, selling his company at the same time as I was. And like me, he was similarly losing his mind about the process. We would text, call, go on walks together, and just essentially bitch about what we were going through. Knowing that someone else was dealing with it and that I wasn't alone was extremely valuable. I could lean on his experience and vice versa to look at our situations differently and come up with solutions. So, look for friends who can support you through situations, even if they aren't entrepreneurs. You already know those friends who are always there for you and pick you up. Make sure they are part of your support system when you need it.

Therapists/Life Coaches

Therapists can play a crucial role in helping entrepreneurs navigate the inherent ups and downs of running a business. They can help address the psychological and emotional challenges you will face as a business owner.

Whether or not you have prior experience with therapists, I highly recommend adding them to your team. When I was dealing with my PTSD as a youth, I had seen a therapist for years, and she was instrumental in me navigating that challenging time in my life. But I had not seen one for the twenty or so years after. Three years into my business, I felt like everything that I was doing was not enough, and I needed additional support. I started seeing a therapist and would sit with her for an hour per week. And this was not a lying-down-on-the-couch-and-let's-talk-about-Mommy-issues type of session; this was more life coaching. Therapists come in all shapes and sizes and can guide you with any challenges you are facing.

And if nothing else, as I joke to my therapist Dr. Sue, they can essentially get paid to hear you bitch for an hour. Many times, I didn't go in there with any specific issue; I just went in there and bitched for an hour and then left. "This person did this and is a moron." "This person fucked up again, and I want to fire them." "Can you believe what this idiot did? What an asshole." I would bitch for an hour and leave, and I felt way better!

You can go with my tried-and-true just-bitch-and-let-it-out strategy, but obviously, therapists also deploy a various number of techniques based on your situation and goals. Some examples are cognitive-behavioral therapy, mindfulness practices, or even narrative therapy. Either way, therapists can help entrepreneurs develop healthier coping mechanisms to manage stress, enhance your emotional resilience, and improve interpersonal skills, which are all crucial for effective leadership and team management.

One of the most significant benefits I gained from therapy was guidance in achieving a better work-life balance as an entrepreneur. I really struggled to stop thinking about work even when I wasn't technically "working." My wife used to say, "I mean, I know you are physically here, but mentally, you are somewhere else." My therapist worked with me on tools and tactics for my transition from the office to home so I could be more present.

One tactic that worked particularly well for me was a practice where when I left the office (where I always felt like I had to be "on" in front of my employees), I would stop in a parking lot for fifteen minutes and just sit there, allowing myself to have some "me time." I would usually listen to music or a humor-based podcast. It allowed me to lower my blood pressure so I wouldn't be all geared up and triggered about whatever happened at work that day. It allowed me to walk into the house in a much more relaxed and friendly state.

Another tactic my therapist gave me was for me to have a mental image of me taking off my "working hat" the minute I got in the door. I used to carry a laptop bag with me every day, so I used the action of putting the laptop bag down as my "taking off my working hat." It was a subtle reminder that I had to shift from CEO to my home life. Once I figured out how to effectively do this, I was a much better (not perfect, but better) husband and dad.

My therapist, Dr. Sue, became a valuable member of my team, and I don't know how I would have gotten through the time of selling the company without her. Don't overlook this incredibly valuable resource you can use. You will perform better at work if you are mentally more stable and happier. You can also gain the huge benefit of little to no out-of-pocket expense, as most therapists are covered by insurance. I can't recommend finding one highly enough. If you want to talk to Dr. Sue specifically, she does provide remote counseling, and I will provide her info in the bonus content you will receive for writing a review.

REMOVING STRESSORS FROM YOUR LIFE

Now that we have looked at some people who can help you, let's look at some actions that can help remove stressors from your life.

Removing Daily Tasks

Finding someone to help with daily tasks related to the business or your personal life can alleviate stress and free up your time to focus on the company. This balance was key to my success. Once again, my primary support system in this area was my wife. Early on, when discussing the business, we agreed that I would pretty much one hundred percent focus on building and running the company, and she would pretty much one hundred percent focus on raising the kids. We decided that to effectively pull this off, she would not go back to work.

My family is and always has been my number one priority. Still, I also know myself and knew that I would have to be "all in" on this business, and my wife needed to understand that. After all, we put our life savings into it, and I was the sole breadwinner. So, whenever it came to signing up the kids for sports, school, or any other activity, my wife took this all on. I didn't need to do anything. This didn't stop me from coaching teams and being involved, but I wasn't responsible for figuring it out.

Another area I learned about removing daily tasks to free up my time was the many automation techniques discussed in *The Four-Hour Work Week*. This book is brilliant at breaking down time-consuming manual activities and developing processes and activities to automate them. Some of the activities I did at the time may seem commonplace now, but at the time, they weren't. Here are a few examples that took little stressors off my plate so I could focus on the business: automating all bills to auto-pay so I didn't have to read mail and write checks, "batching" mail where I wouldn't open it up for a month or so and then go through it all once a month, outsourcing time-consuming activities to overseas companies for a few dollars an hour for tasks such as research, putting together lists, and reaching out to utility companies to lower personal bills. These little things add up and provide mental relief.

Financial Stability

Financial stability is another critical area where you can be supported, especially in contributing to household income or just understanding the financial uncertainties inherent in the early stages of a business. My wife and I agreed that she wouldn't work to focus on the kids, but I needed to talk to her about setting expectations and sticking to our budget. We had a frank conversation ahead of time about how the way we spent money would change in the beginning. We would have a set monthly budget for the first time. This meant cutting back on certain luxuries, such as going out to lunch with friends.

I use this specific example because it became a situation and a conversation we had to have early on. I explained to my wife that I knew how she was accustomed to it but that going out to lunch with friends was out of the question in the first months of starting the company. Then, in the first month, she went out to lunch with friends and spent around $40, and I lost my mind (which I am not proud of). I remember her saying, "Jesus. What did I sign up for?" When running a company, especially in the beginning, little situations like that can seem like a big deal due to all the stress and uncertainty you face daily.

After I calmed down, we talked more, and I explained to her why it was important to me to stick to the budget. In that conversation, I said something to her that became our mantra for the beginning of the business regarding the financial sacrifices we were going to make, and it also served as a reminder that these sacrifices would lead to something great down the line. I said to her, "Short-term sacrifice for a long-term gain." Whenever she complained about us cutting back on things we did before, I would repeat this mantra, "Short-term sacrifice for a long-term gain." I knew it annoyed the shit out of her every time I said it, but she also understood and adopted. Years later, when I sold seventy percent of the business, and the life-changing money came into our bank account, I held up the phone, showed her the bank balance, smiled at her, and said, "Long-term gain." This time, she smiled back.

Having that upfront conversation and being on the same page so you can maintain financial stability will significantly enhance your mindset and better set yourself and your business up for success.

PREVENTING BURNOUT

Whether things are going well or not, the long hours and emotional toll of being an entrepreneur can lead to burnout. Let's now look at some items to help you combat burnout so you can perform at your peak.

Regular Work Breaks

I only took one fifteen-minute break at lunchtime, where I would make a protein shake, close my door, and read ten minutes of Chicago sports articles. That was typically good for me. It provided a bit of a mental break, but I also wanted to get as much done during the workday as possible so I could spend more time with my family at night. You may need more or less, but that worked for me. Anything beyond thirty minutes would start to produce anxiety where whatever I was doing, I would start thinking about work. For instance, I would NEVER go out to lunch unless it was business-related, like meeting with a customer or a potential new employee. Otherwise, it felt like a waste of time, but maybe you would find it different.

Vacations

In the early years, I would sparingly go on vacations, and when I did, I worked most of the time. As I went on through the years, I learned to prioritize vacations. Eventually, I got to the point where I would completely unplug from the business and not look at a single email. I used to joke that it would give me another six months of sprinting when I got back to the company. Dan used to suggest that I go on vacation whenever I felt overly stressed or overwhelmed. He used to say to me, "You don't feel like giving up. You are tired and need a vacation. Vacations are a cure-all." Per usual, he was right. It doesn't mean you need to go on exotic vacations right away—that will happen later, but in the beginning, getting a break and recharging your batteries will propel you forward.

Dedicated Family Time

Integrating dedicated family time into your routines can help you disconnect from your multitude of business responsibilities and reconnect with your personal life. This, for me continually reminded me of my original motivations for starting the company in the first place. I would often feel completely overwhelmed by whatever was going on, and it would all melt away when I saw one of my kids smile or laugh. It puts things in perspective and allows you to re-ground yourself. I also found that after I had this time, I could return to my tasks with renewed energy and clarity, often finding I was more creative and productive as a result.

I found that having a specific schedule with family time carved out was helpful and was a routine I was able to adhere to. Additionally, it gave my wife the benefit of knowing when we could talk and discuss what we needed to, avoiding those conversations during the workday when I had less time. Here is what my daily schedule used to look like for the first four years or so of the business:

- **7 am**: Wake up and say goodbye to kids before they go to school.
- **8 am–6 pm**: Dedicated work time. Full go and heads down with minimal breaks.
- **6 pm–8:30 pm**: Dedicated family time. Spend time with kids outdoors, play sports, go on walks, make and have dinner, and get kids to bed.
- **8:30 pm–10 pm**: Dedicated time with my wife. Typically, we watch a TV show or movie together, talk, or hang out outside and relax.
- **10 pm–2 am or so**: Wife goes to bed. For me, it was the time for overflow work, responding to emails, and quiet time to think strategically about bigger decisions. Typically, this was the most productive time and when I got my best work done. I felt energized from the time with the family but also anxious to get things done that I had thought of over the past few hours and couldn't wait until the morning. I would always listen to music (Sirius XM Chill was and still is my favorite) and crank out my work.

You should create a similar calendar. It will give you some sense of control in an otherwise overwhelmingly chaotic time. Carving out dedicated family time was incredibly helpful for me, my loved ones, and my business. It's easy to get caught up in your own BS and put family time aside. I am here to tell you: Don't. This is a time you will not be able to make up, and it will be something you regret if you do.

IN CONCLUSION

Are you tired yet? We just had an exhausting workout. You should be nice and sweaty. I promise you these exercises will give you the strength to overcome anything.

Looking back at these last chapters, we can see we covered a lot. We discussed developing an entrepreneurial mindset, where we learned to embrace risk and uncertainty. We talked about building resilience practices to deal with the inevitable setbacks. Lastly, we discussed building the community and the tactics needed to help you along the way. Business success comes down to the people in the business; you, as the business owner and leader, are the most important person. So, spend the time and energy on yourself. I promise you it will pay dividends inside and outside of the business.

PHASE FIVE
BUILDING THE BUSINESS—THE CUSTOMER

In this phase, we will discuss how to build and maintain a successful business. We will discuss the importance and strategies for building a customer-centric business, all with key lessons and stories I learned along the way. We will also dive into how to build winning products and services for your customers and, once you do, how to protect them.

CHAPTER 13
BUILDING A CUSTOMER-CENTRIC BUSINESS MODEL

 The most important single thing is to focus obsessively on the customer.

JEFF BEZOS, FOUNDER AND FORMER CEO OF AMAZON

Placing customers at the heart of a business model should be the focus permeating every facet of decision-making inside and outside your company. Sustaining success in business is incredibly difficult. On the surface most will think it is achieved through the products or services a company offers. I am here to tell you that is false. Sustainable success is all about the experiences and value you deliver to your customers. Therefore you must learn to develop a customer-centric business model. This model disrupts the traditional paradigms of the past, shifting from a focus on product innovation to customer satisfaction and loyalty.

This customer-centric focus was at the heart of everything we did at my company. I always told my team that they didn't work for Controle—they worked for our customers, and the money flowed through Controle. As you can see below, anyone who entered my office was greeted with an "Our Boss" picture. This picture had several of our customers' logos to remind them that even though I was the CEO, I was not their real boss. Additionally, I told them that if I called them and they were on the phone with a client, they should ignore my call because the customer was more important than me.

Of course, we were not alone in this customer-first philosophy. Many companies have adopted a customer-centric business model and have achieved great success. Let's look at a few now. You are likely already one of their customers.

EXAMPLES OF SUCCESSFUL CUSTOMER-CENTRIC COMPANIES

1. **Amazon**: Amazon has set the standard for a customer-centric business model. Its commitment to customer satisfaction is evident through services like Amazon Prime, which initially provided free shipping but continues to increase its value to customers with additional services such as video streaming and unlimited photo storage. Additionally, it was one of the first companies to adopt a no-stress return shipping policy. Further, Amazon was one of the first e-commerce companies to nail using customer data to improve the shopping experience, making recommendations based on your past purchases and browsing habits. I don't know about you, but

from a customer perspective, I love Amazon. Whenever I look to buy anything, I start on Amazon.com. I know that it will get to my house fast and if there are problems, they will take care of it.

2. **Zappos**: Known for its exceptional customer service, Zappos has built its brand around customer satisfaction. The company offers a 365-day return policy and 24/7 customer service. Zappos empowers its employees to go the extra mile to make customers happy, which includes sending flowers or pizza to customers as a gesture of goodwill. If you want to learn more about how they did it, read the excellent book *Delivering Happiness* by their late Founder and CEO, Tony Hsieh. They used this customer-centric approach to great success, which led to their eventual purchase by Amazon for over one billion dollars.

3. **Netflix**: Netflix has revolutionized the entertainment industry with its customer-centric approach. Netflix came up with their entire service by meeting with customers and understanding their frustrations with the current process of renting DVDs from brick-and-mortar stores like Blockbuster. Additionally, by leveraging data analytics, Netflix offers personalized content recommendations based on your viewing habits. The company's focus on customer preferences is also evident in its original content production, which often targets niche audiences and is all backed up by the data it gathers on its customer's viewing habits.

These companies demonstrate how a customer-centric approach can increase customer satisfaction and loyalty, ultimately leading to their business's success. By consistently prioritizing the customer's needs and preferences, these companies have enhanced their competitive edge and fostered strong emotional connections with their customers. Now, let's look at the core elements of having a customer-centric approach.

PRINCIPLE 1: GET INTO THE MIND OF YOUR CUSTOMER

 To train zee dolphin, you must zink like zee dolphin! You must be getting inside zee dolphin's head. I am saying to Snowflake, "Akay! Akay Akay Akay?" and he is saying, "Akay Akay!" and he is up on zee tail, "Eeeeeeeee!" and you can quote him!

ACE VENTURA, PRESIDENT OF ACE VENTURA PET DETECTIVE

Jesus, did this guy really quote Ace Ventura in a business book? Has this man no shame?

The first step in developing a customer-centric business model is to get into your customers' minds and shoes. You must understand their goals and objectives, pains and frustrations, and especially what keeps them up at night. There are several ways to do this, each with different pros and cons; let's look at some now.

Interviews

In my opinion and experience, there's no better way to understand your customers and craft winning solutions than by sitting down and talking with them. After I had created my business plan and come up with what I believed would be winning solutions, I wanted to test my hypothesis, so I asked some of my customers with whom I had been through the process of selling and implementing the solution previously. I was confident I knew the challenges but wanted to hear directly from them.

The first customer I met was my buddy Neal Hemenover, whom I had been working with for a few years, and we got along great. I knew he was a no-bullshit type of guy who would give it to me straight, which I appreciated. I asked him to lunch and told him I was thinking about starting a business around what he had been through and wanted to hear about his experience. He walked me through what he felt went well and what didn't. Then he asked me what I was thinking about regarding services, listened, and nodded his head along to most of everything.

After I was done, I asked him, "What service did I NOT describe that you think would be valuable?" He perked up and said, "What you really need is a service that bridges the gap between the IT and legal people. IT people hate dealing with lawyers, and lawyers hate dealing with IT people. IT people don't want to deal with this problem, and the lawyers can't figure it out on their own. So, if you had an offering that would bridge that gap, I would buy it." BAM, TOUCHDOWN! Here was a customer telling me precisely what he wanted and that he would buy it. This conversation led to my first product offering; I even named it "Bridge the Gap." As of writing this, twelve years later, that service is still one of the company's most popular and profitable services.

You might wonder what type of questions you should ask in these interviews. It's less about asking specific questions and more about getting them to describe their experiences and frustrations. You want to use open-ended questions.

Here are some questions you would ask about what they are currently dealing with:

- Can you tell me about ...?
- Can you walk me through how you ... ?
- Walk me through what went right and what didn't ... ?

Here are some questions you can ask to learn how they like to purchase from companies:

- When choosing a vendor in this space, what do you look for?
- Think about your favorite service provider. Can you please tell me what separates them from the rest?

Here are some you can use to ascertain what they think about daily:

- What do you talk to colleagues in your industry the most about?
- What magazines or podcasts do you subscribe to?
- What sites do you go to most often?
- What are the things that keep you up at night?

Once you understand the customer's likes, dislikes, goals, and objectives, you can consider how to help them solve these issues. Think through what you would do to solve them if you worked at their company. You will be in an advantageous position in that you can come up with creative solutions to their problems, ones that they likely would have not come up with on their own.

Online Surveys

The challenge with sit-down interviews is that not everyone will give you one. People's time is valuable, and often, an interview is not feasible, or they will cancel you at the last minute when an inevitable work emergency arises. So, you must get creative to hear your customer's voice directly. Another way to do this effectively is by using online surveys. The main goal of surveys is not to glean deep insights. That is for the interviews. The survey's purpose is to validate your understanding of what you have already discovered.

Regarding tools, we used SurveyMonkey, which provides a very easy-to-use and customizable web survey to gather and distill information. When designing solutions for customers, we would shoot for five in-person interviews. Then, we would try to hear from another twenty people using surveys. The key to surveys is for them to be short and succinct. We would aim for them to be five questions or less and for them to be completed in less than one minute.

Further, we would tell those we sent the online survey that one minute was the time commitment, so they weren't left guessing. People have small attention spans, so make it easy for them. We found the success rate for completion shot up dramatically when we told them how long it took to complete. It's hard to argue about doing something that takes sixty seconds to finish, especially if people feel they will benefit or feel internal pressure to get it done.

Additionally, the survey's format is essential. Typically, we would provide two to three multiple-choice questions. Then, we would have a few open-ended questions and leave a blank field for them to write in a response. I suggest doing it in this order because if you can get them to answer the first few questions quickly and easily, they are more likely to finish the open-ended survey questions. If all the questions are open-ended, they might open the link, think, *I don't have time for this*, and close it. We found our success rate went up when the first answers were multiple choice.

Finally, using tools like SurveyMonkey, you can easily aggregate the responses and get them in a format that you can use to summarize the results and look for trends. It's another valuable tool for getting inside your customers' heads so you can build winning solutions for them.

Market Research and Insights

Another practice to get inside your customer's head is to use market research to gather insights about customer preferences, market trends, and competitors' actions. I constantly kept up with industry trends and other companies in our arena. A few years into the company, we signed up with Gartner, the leading IT market research company. I would talk to the analysts in our industry monthly to hear what they were hearing from their customers. We then took this information and built solutions around it. I remember one customer saying to me when we presented a new solution, "It's like you read my mind. This is exactly what we are looking for, and it does not exist." I didn't read her mind; I just had the market research from Gartner telling me what people were struggling with.

Analytics

Another practical approach to get inside the customer's head is to use analytics to understand what they are searching for and what content is resonating with them. You can then use that information to double down on what is working. Using tools like Google Analytics on your website can give you a sense of what is happening in the customer's head. Every week, I used Google Analytics to track which web pages had the most visits, how long users stayed on those pages, and which content had the highest engagement. Additionally, for e-commerce companies, you can do what Amazon did and use tools to track user behavior and purchasing habits to know what to invest further in.

Another tactic in this space is to use and monitor social media platforms to understand the engagement and sentiment of your posts. By using native tools like Facebook Insights or Twitter analytics, you can get an idea of what content is resonating and what is not. Recently, I created an Instagram page for a movie I am producing (more on this later), and by using Instagram's analytics, I can see what people like and share the most. I then use that information to make sure that the content is in the final movie. Using these built-in tools gives you a better sense of what is inside your customer's head.

PRINCIPLE 2: TAKE CARE OF THE CUSTOMER AT ALL COSTS

You likely have a story about a company that went above and beyond for you and how that made you feel. Unfortunately, you also likely have a story about a horrible customer experience and how that made you feel. Just think to yourself: After going through those, how likely were you to work with that company again? Exactly.

You will want to instill a culture in your company that makes it clear that the customer comes first all day, every day and that you will do whatever it takes to take care of them. I will get more into how we instilled this at my company in the culture chapter, but this cannot be overstated. I don't care what type of company you have; you will have competitors who will do what you do. What can really separate you is simply the level of care you give to your customers. Do you think Zappos is the only company that sells shoes?

I saw firsthand the long-term benefits of taking care of a customer at any cost in the months before I started the company. A year before I left EMC, I sold a customer a deal in December. Often, in tech sales jobs, your customers from the year prior are taken away from you, and you won't work with them the following year. This was the case with this customer. In February of the following year, they went to implement the solution, and it was a DISASTER. Everything seemed to be going wrong. My key contact with the customer, Steve Marcolini, felt stuck, and he called me desperately, asking me to help him. Even though he was not my customer any more, I told him I would help him figure it out. With all my customers, I wanted them to be successful with whatever I sold them, and I took it personally if they weren't.

I called around internally, and no one wanted to help him. The new sales rep knew the customer wouldn't buy anything for years and told me he wouldn't help. What a fucking clown. The sales manager was too busy to help and didn't give a shit. The internal services team had outsourced the installation to a partner, so they essentially washed their hands of it. So, for the next several months, I continued to spend time ensuring this solution was successfully implemented for Steve. It was excruciating, and I was on many long calls that took me away from my day job. But I didn't care because it was in my DNA to help the customer. I always felt customers had to trust me to buy from me, and I wanted to prove them right. Eventually, we got it all taken care of, and Steve was incredibly appreciative of all that I did.

Six months later, when I was getting ready to launch the business, I called Steve and said, "Hey, I'm thinking about leaving and starting a company doing services around what you went through. Can I bend your ear on it?" Before I even got another word out, he said, "Sign me up to be your first customer." I was floored. I jokingly said to him, "But you don't even know what I am doing yet." He continued, "I don't care. You took care of my problem even though there was nothing in it for you. Those are the type of people I like to surround myself with in business." And he stuck to his word. He was indeed one of my first customers, and he signed up for our managed service for every single one of the ten years of the company and continues to this day. He continued looking for projects to work on with my company and always gave us opportunities. THAT is what taking care of your customer and treating them like royalty does.

PRINCIPLE 3: GET TO KNOW THEM PERSONALLY

Many people feel they need to separate their business and personal lives. I don't agree with that at all. When running a business, the two are intertwined whether you like it or not. So, embrace it. In the beginning, I did, and as we expanded, I always encouraged our team to get to know our customers personally. We found that engaging with them outside of the workplace was the easiest way to do this. Take them out to lunch. Take them out to dinner. Take them to a sports event or concert. Take them to do whatever they like doing. And then don't talk about business. Just get to know them personally. Know their likes and dislikes, hobbies, where they grew up, and about their children and family. I promise you this will go a very, very long way. In return, they will get to know you and will be more willing to take chances on you and your business if they do. We all want to do business with people we like and trust. Also, it has the added benefit of being a ton of fun! I made so many good, genuine friends and had so many fun experiences through this approach, and it is one of the few things I miss about working in Corporate America now that I am retired. Additionally, often, these customers become the ones you can call on to be a reference or pick their brains when thinking about a new solution.

PRINCIPLE 4: MAKE IT EASY TO DO BUSINESS WITH YOUR COMPANY

Let's face it: People are generally lazy. No one likes roadblocks put in their way, and if there are significant roadblocks, they will look for an easier path. When you are fortunate enough to have a customer choose your company, you better make it as easy as possible for them to do business with you. The challenge with B2B transactions is that when two companies have never done business before, you must establish legal agreements and accounting paperwork before you can start working together. This process, many times, can be painful.

While this paperwork is necessary, it is also essential to make sure there are many eyes on getting through the process as quickly and painlessly as possible for the customer or risk that they will go elsewhere. We constantly looked at our paperwork to strip it down to the fewest legalities possible and make it as fair as possible to both parties. Early on, as I took advice from our attorneys, the first versions of our contracts were way too one-sided to protect my company and not the customer. After the first few go-rounds of using these agreements and seeing the edits and comments from customers, I could see that this approach was straight-up pissing them off. One even told me, "Let's just stop right now. My legal team will never approve this; we are not doing business together." That was an eye-opener for me. I quickly pivoted to working with my attorneys to understand the essential elements and make the agreements fair to both sides right from the get-go. That was a more practical approach, and that was how it would result anyway.

Additionally, we worked diligently with our customers' accounting teams to get whatever info they needed ASAP and do it in a friendly manner. Eventually, how your people treat their people will be relayed, so make sure it's a positive impression.

Although we did not have a B2C practice, I have dealt with this in my personal life. Quick pay options such as Apple Pay, PayPal, and others have made it much easier for people to buy your products, and implementing tools like that goes a long way. I have often seen something online that I wanted to buy, and then I added it to my cart and tried to pay. If none of these quick pay options were available and I had to manually enter my credit card, but my wallet wasn't in sight, I would simply move on without buying it. So, make it easy for customers to transact business with your company, or they will find someone else who will.

PRINCIPLE 5: GET FEEDBACK

The last step in the customer-centric model is to get feedback from them. It's not good enough to instill into your team that they need to do all the right things for the customer; you must go back to the customer and ensure they are. Getting customer feedback is much easier early in the business as you will be close to them. However, as time goes on and the company grows, hearing directly from them will become increasingly difficult unless something is going very wrong. Then you will definitely hear from them.

One effective way to do this is using customer feedback surveys. After every engagement we did with our customers, we would send them a five-question customer satisfaction survey, and we used SurveyMonkey to do it. As I mentioned, we found that five was the magic number to get them to respond. These were the exact questions that we asked:

1. Did your sales representative understand your needs and provide you with appropriate service options?
2. Please rate your satisfaction with Controle's delivery team (one being lowest, ten being highest):
3. Would you work with Controle again and recommend them to peers?
4. For what other initiatives would you consider working with Controle? Please check all that apply:
   - We then listed out five categories of services with brief descriptions
   - Additionally, this shows that these surveys can be used both to get customer feedback and for marketing purposes. We found many opportunities out of this question.
5. Would you be willing to be a Controle customer reference?

Early in rolling this out, we found that we were getting a low response rate. So, to increase it, we held both the sales and delivery teams responsible for receiving a response and provided an incentive to the customer. We told them that if they responded, we would either give them a $25 Amazon gift card or make a $25 donation to the charity of their choice. This second option is important as some customers will have rules on receiving gifts from vendors or feel uncomfortable doing so. Providing this incentive to respond significantly increased the percentage of responses.

Once you get the responses, you have to review them. I read every single one, and they made my day in many instances. I found it incredibly invigorating to read our customers' feedback. The most valuable thing you can hear in business is customer feedback. If one was particularly helpful or detailed, I would email the customer and personally thank them for taking the time out of their busy day. I highly recommend gathering feedback from customers.

In summary, making the customer the heart of everything your company stands for is a surefire way to ensure its success. If there were a single thing you focused on to assure success, this would be it. The customer is always everyone's boss. It's up to you to be hired or fired.

CHAPTER 14
PRODUCT DEVELOPMENT —BUILDING WINNING PRODUCTS AND SOLUTIONS

> *You've got to start with the customer experience and work backward to the technology.*
>
> STEVE JOBS, CO-FOUNDER AND CEO OF APPLE

Product development is the output of combining many of the things we have learned so far. From idea-generation techniques to testing and validating these ideas, a customer-centric point of view, branding, and marketing, it is a conglomeration of many instrumental individual parts of the business.

This chapter will discuss the high-level components of crafting and bringing products to market. Further, I highly recommend you read a few books outside of *The Blueprint* regarding product development, as it is a deep and broad subject. The first one I recommend starting with is *The Lean Startup* by Eric Riehs, and the second is *Crossing the Chasm* by Geoffrey Moore. They were inspirational and helped lead much of our product development efforts at Controle. In this chapter, in addition to describing the real-world experience we gathered, I will summarize the lessons we learned from these books and other books. Further, I will add lessons from a Pragmatic Marketing product development training and certification that many of our team went through and found helpful.

ELEMENTS FOR A SUCCESSFUL PRODUCT CREATION AND LAUNCH

Product development generally includes several vital elements to ensure a product's successful creation and launch. Let's look at them now:

Idea Generation

Go back to Chapter 3, where we discussed various ways to create ideas for your business. These are also the same for developing a winning product or solution. Remember, for our customers, we are either looking to decrease pain or increase pleasure. Then, similarly to what we did for the company idea, we put it through the same test on the market viability of the solution.

Concept Development and Evaluation

Once we have developed some ideas, we want to get them in front of potential customers as soon as humanly possible to elicit feedback. This is the "does anyone care" test. It can be as simple as asking for a phone call with a customer or expert in the solution you are trying to solve, telling them what you are thinking about doing, and seeing what they say.

When developing the concept, you will also want to assess the product's technical, financial, and operational feasibility. Work with your internal teams or outside consultants to determine what it will take to bring it to market and ensure it can be manufactured at scale.

Business Analysis

There are three main elements you will want to think through when building the business case for the product. They are as follows:

1. **Cost Estimation**: Here, you will calculate the costs of developing and producing the product. This can include materials, outside companies helping make it, and internal

labor costs. Also, it's more categorized as a "soft cost," but there is always an opportunity cost to building new products or solutions, or in other words, a cost for people working on this versus something else they could be working on. These soft costs need to be evaluated as well.
2. **Pricing Strategy**: This is the step for determining the optimal pricing model for the product. Look at how others are pricing similar solutions in the market and weigh any different or better features you or your competitors have and the potential increase or decrease in value you can charge versus competitors. Or consider using a value-based pricing approach, in which you price it out not on how others are charging but rather based on how much value your customers will receive from it.
3. **Sales Forecasting**: This is where you will project potential sales volumes and revenue. Like the exercise in the business plan, we will want to gauge what first-year sales can look like, be realistic, and back it up with data.

Once you have considered all these elements, calculate the return on investment (ROI) timeline. Then, further explore whether this product or solution can open opportunities for your other products and solutions, which should also be considered in the ROI calculation.

Project Management

Once you determine your product or solution is green-lit, set and adhere to development timelines and milestones. Have a dedicated project manager for individual components or a dedicated product manager who will be responsible for the product's overall success. Due to the size of our organization, this person was one and the same. Make sure these people ensure that the necessary resources (team, budget, tools) are available and effectively utilized.

Product Design and Development

Per the lessons learned in *The Lean Startup*, we will want to create a prototype or a minimum viable product (MVP) to test the concept. You don't need a polished solution or product to do this. When we developed our two in-house software solutions, we had customers in and looking at it early on. Embarrassingly so early on. In the case of the first software product we created, a customer was literally in the room when we were whiteboarding the initial concept. Once you get the MVP in front of customers, refine and iterate the product design based on their feedback and testing results. Then, do it again and again and again until you get close to a finished solution.

Testing and Validation

Once you have the product or solution close to what you feel is market-ready, get it in front of users who will use it, and ideally, not the same ones who have been exposed to it in the MVP stage. Don't give them any training or instruction; give it to them and see how they can navigate it. Observe what they do and solicit feedback on what worked and what didn't. Further, rigorous internal testing must be performed to identify defects and issues. We had our internal team of consultants who were technical but didn't have experience with our software product, essentially trying to break it. Then, we identified specific individuals who became responsible for resolving all the issues we identified, so nothing slipped through the cracks.

Marketing Strategy

In a few chapters, we will talk about branding. The first step for marketing is identifying the product or solution's brand identity and messaging. Then, as we discussed in the business plan chapter, consider how to identify your target market and how you will go after it. Finally, figure out what distribution methods (social media or otherwise) we discussed in the business plan chapter on what will be most effective.

Launch Planning

Coordinate and document all launch activities, which are many, for a successful product launch. Pick a specific date (it WILL slip many times) and write down all the tasks you need to complete to get there. Have a green, yellow, and red-light dashboard you can review weekly to make sure you are on track.

Post-Launch Review and Support

Track the product's market performance by collecting customer feedback using the tactics we discussed in the customer-centric business model chapter. Use this feedback to make necessary adjustments and improvements. Further, identify what is needed to provide ongoing support to customers, whether it be documentation, personnel, or both, to ensure satisfaction and address any issues. Identify what resources you will need to field customer calls or emails.

Regulatory and Compliance

If applicable, ensure the product meets all relevant regulations and standards. Further, protect the product through patents, trademarks, or copyrights, which we will discuss in the next chapter.

In conclusion, success in business comes down to how much value you can provide and how well you take care of your customers. By constantly looking through the customer's lens, soliciting and incorporating their feedback, and having a clearly laid-out plan to get the product from idea to market, your products and your company will be set up for success.

CHAPTER 15
INTELLECTUAL PROPERTY 101

Now that we have developed these brilliant ideas, proven them out with our customers, and are making traction, we need to protect them. Creating and protecting intellectual property (IP) is important for safeguarding these innovations and fortifying your market position.

Navigating the intricate domain of IP rights requires understanding its various forms. Each option serves as a blockade against potential encroachment by your competitors while simultaneously offering you strategic positioning in the marketplace. This section is meant to give you a high-level understanding of the options and what they specifically aim to protect for you.

IP can be protected in various ways depending on what it is. Distinguishing between patents, trademarks, copyrights, and trade secrets unveils many legal protections for your ideas. Let's look at them now.

PATENTS

A patent is a form of IP that grants the patent holder exclusive rights to an invention for a certain period, typically twenty years from the filing date, in exchange for public disclosure. The exclusive rights include excluding others from making, using, selling, or importing the patented invention without permission. While obtaining a patent can be time-consuming and expensive, if successful, it can be extremely valuable. There are three types of patents: utility, design, and plant.

Utility Patents

Utility patents cover new and useful inventions or discoveries of processes, machines, articles of manufacture, compositions of matter, or improvements to any of these. Think of something that didn't exist before but now does. Alexander Graham Bell's telephone and Thomas Edison's lightbulb are famous examples.

Design Patents

Design patents protect new, original, and ornamental designs for an article of manufacture. A famous design patent is the iPhone. Apple didn't make the telephone; they just improved its design.

Plant Patents

Plant patents are granted for new and distinct, invented, or discovered asexually reproduced plants. For example, a number of apples, like the Red Delicious and Honeycrisp, have specific patents on them, which I had no clue about until researching for this book!

Patents are a particularly nuanced field, and if you think you have something patentable, discuss it with a patent attorney. Many books and other resources are also available that more specifically discuss this fascinating area of business. At my company, we never attempted to get a patent, so unfortunately, I don't have many personal anecdotes to share here.

TRADEMARKS

A trademark is a distinctive sign, design, word, phrase, symbol, or combination that identifies and distinguishes the goods or services of one entity from those of others. It serves as a brand identifier that helps consumers recognize and differentiate products or services in the marketplace.

You can easily identify if something is trademarked if it has that little "R" or "TM" on part of the logo or brand. For my company, we had multiple trademarks. The way I looked at trademarks was that they are essentially a way to tell competitors, "Hey, don't use my product names or terms; they are mine." The first one I did was the company name Controle. For obvious reasons, I didn't want my competitors to use the term "controle" in the context of our industry. That would have been confusing to our customers.

The second trademark I filed was for our product offering, Bridge the Gap, which we discussed in the customer-centric model chapter. I knew it was a brilliant name, especially since it came from a customer, and I knew I would be able to tell that origin story. I also knew my competitors would probably try to copy it, and they eventually did. It deserved protection.

I did those two in year one. Later, we also filed trademarks for our in-house developed software tools, which we discussed in the last chapter. We used LegalZoom to register all of them, and it was a straightforward process. Below is what my Controle trademark looked like—notice the little "R" in the corner. That signified to the market that it was "registered" and to back off, buster, or else.

COPYRIGHT

Copyright is a form of IP protection that gives creators exclusive rights to their original works of authorship, such as literature (books), music, art, and software. Copyrights prohibit others from reproducing it, distributing it, or derivative works without the owner's consent, ensuring you have control over your creations.

Copyrights are simple to understand. If a band creates an amazing song, they don't want anyone to randomly be able to throw it online and sell it without the band getting paid. The band has a copyright on their song, protecting the hard work they put into creating it.

For my company, we had two copyrights on the two software products we created. We didn't want people copying our software and selling it independently. Additionally, this book is copyrighted. I worked my ass off on this book, so I don't want someone to copy and paste, change the name of the book (maybe the Redprint, perhaps?), and sell it. Ok, I know that is dramatic and probably not realistic, but you get the idea. Copyrights protect you from others stealing your original work.

TRADE SECRETS

A trade secret is a type of IP comprising highly confidential and proprietary information that gives a business a competitive advantage. Trade secrets can include formulas, practices, processes, designs, instruments, patterns, or information compilations that others do not generally know or are reasonably ascertainable.

Unlike patents, trade secrets are not publicly disclosed. They can be protected indefinitely if they remain secret and provide economic value to the business. Additionally, trade secrets differ from the others in that they are not registered with any government authority. Instead, they are protected through confidentiality agreements and security measures within a business.

A famous example of a trade secret is the recipe for Coca-Cola. Coke doesn't want anyone to know how they make it, as others could steal and repurpose it. Some other famous ones are Google's search algorithm and McDonald's Big Mac Special sauce (it's just mayo and mustard combined, right?)

Similarly to patents, trade secrets are an incredibly nuanced field. If you think you have some "special sauce" to what you're doing (see what I did there?), and it's unique to you and you only, and you want to protect it, you should speak to an IP attorney. Unfortunately, I don't have many personal anecdotes to share here as we didn't have any highly confidential information that provided us significant value to the business. Besides, of course, the fact that customers love Yeti company mascots will keep your Yeti tchotchkes on their desks, reminding them of your company every day and making them more likely to call you. You will hear more about this later in the branding chapter. But well, shit, the cat is out of the bag on that secret now. Does anyone know how I delete this part from the book?

In conclusion, IP can help you protect your ideas and gain a competitive edge in the marketplace. It's not easy to come up with winning ideas or creations, so if you do, make sure they are protected. It will help you sleep at night.

PHASE SIX
BUILDING THE BUSINESS—THE COMPANY

Now that we have looked at the customer, we will now turn our focus internally to our company, building out the team and ensuring sustained success. We will talk about how to define and create company culture. Further we will discuss some key strategies around the key elements of how to keep opportunity and money coming in the door: branding, marketing, and sales.

CHAPTER 16
USE THE FORCE—COMPANY CULTURE AS THE HEARTBEAT OF THE BUSINESS

At the company's beginning, your focus will need to be solely on pure survival and doing whatever it takes to get to the next quarter. Eventually, you WILL get past this "scary phase," which for us was about halfway through our second year, when we were really humming. Once you do, you will want to shift your focus to look internally and build up the company for sustained long-term success. There is no better way to do that than by focusing on that often-talked-about but commonly misunderstood concept: company culture.

But what is "company culture" exactly? First, understand that it is an invisible yet undeniable force. It is a force that acts as the heartbeat of the business and serves as its personality. It propels innovation, fosters unity among your team, and helps your company sustain growth. Culture weaves its way through the everyday interactions, decision-making processes, and shared traits that underpin a company's identity. But in the beginning, it is common for things to move so fast and have your focus elsewhere that the company culture just happens without anyone noticing or talking about it.

So, how do we then hit pause and define or create company culture? The genesis of a strong culture begins with clarity—a clear definition of your company's mission, values, and convictions. Your team needs to understand what you stand for before they can even think about following your lead. Once you define your culture, you can work to embed these principles into everyday business operations.

The easiest way I can explain how to develop and cultivate company culture is to walk you through how we did at Controle, which is what these lessons will surround in this chapter. When I started thinking more about defining our culture, I looked at it through two lenses: 1) What I wanted the company to be and 2) What the company was already. Then, I went through an exercise to help document what these were and how best to shape them in the future.

COMPANY CHARACTERISTICS

I started with a list of my own personality traits that I felt were critical to my success. I then identified and pinpointed the traits of the most successful people at the company and the types of folks I wanted to be a part of the team going forward. I then combined these two lists into one. Here is what it looked like.

Competencies/Traits of the most successful people

- Self motivated
- Talented
- Team player
- Customer focused
- Helpful
- Goal oriented
- Intelligent
- Honesty/integrity
- Strong work ethic
- Openness to ideas
- Prideful
- Ambitious

- Follow through
- Good communicator
- Attention to detail
- Proactive
- Persistent
- Cool, calm and collective
- Creative
- Fun
- High standards
- Someone who wants to Take Control of their life!

Further, I then looked at what we had built in the first two years and wrote down what I felt were the company's characteristics. I planned to get all of this down and then present it to everyone. I felt that documenting it would crystallize with our team what we were and were not about. As I put it together, I spoke to several folks on the team to get their take. There was a lot of agreement, and they also added other characteristics and traits that I then added to the lists. I then presented it to the entire company, and whenever new employees came on board going forward, I personally walked them through all of it as part of their onboarding process. Here is what it looked like.

Characteristics of Controle

- **Customer Focused**
  - Take care of the customer's problem and they will take care of yours
- **Results Oriented**
  - Style doesn't matter, results do. What's working (emphasize) and what's not working (adjust). It's that simple.
- **Sales Led (sorry ☺)**
- **Market Driven**
  - What are our customers looking for (be on the lookout)
- **Ambitious**
- **Entrepreneurial**
- **Always evolving, never sitting idle**
- **Not always easy but you won't ever be bored!**

For the company characteristics, let's break down the items one by one, explaining what they mean and how I explained them to the team.

Customer-Focused: By now, you should know how I feel about being customer-focused. I made sure that everyone we added to our team was the same. We made this focus a large part of our interviews, and we would always have them give us examples of how they cared for their customers in their previous jobs. We only hired people who were obsessed with this or who were a customer already and knew how we rolled. Further, there was a reason why this component was first on the list. I wanted everyone to know the ranking of items. The customer is and always should be first.

Results-Oriented: As mentioned, I come from a sales background. The beauty of sales is in its simplicity for its definition of success. It is simply about having a goal (sales quota) and whether you achieved it or not. Sales jobs don't care about what you look like, your race, sex, and or religion. They also don't care if you play the corporate ladder game and or politick. It's all about whether you achieved your targeted results or not, and there are no excuses. For me, I just wanted to be judged on performance and not some other circumstantial BS. Therefore, having a results-oriented job like sales was perfect for me.

When we were hiring, we looked for people with similar results-oriented traits—people who wanted to be judged based on the merits of their work and nothing else. We would look for people who discussed their ability to hit their goals and wanted clarity about what success would look like and how they would be measured against it.

Sales-Led: There are different types of company classifications, and they all have distinct cultures. "Sales-led" companies or companies driven by sales or sales leaders focus on revenue being the number one driver of the company. Additionally, they tend to be hard-charging, a bit loose on company operations, and fun. These types of organizations love performance metrics, and the salespeople typically are the main drivers of the relationship with the customer. As mentioned, it is more important to take a healthy look in the mirror, understand what you are and what you are not, and then own it. It might have made some people uncomfortable, particularly those in our engineering group, but we were sales-led and not shy about it.

Market-Driven: Being market-driven requires a high degree of adaptability. Companies must be agile and able to pivot their strategies based on market feedback and changes. The world changes every single day, and in business, it is absolutely critical to have the courage and flexibility to move with it. If you don't, I promise you that your company will be left behind.

This flexibility to be market-driven can involve adjusting, redesigning products, or shifting service models as needed. This certainly can be scary for companies, especially if you are succeeding. The more successful the company becomes, the harder it becomes to be agile and flexible. However, I instilled embracing change into the company's fabric and routinely pushed people out of their comfort zones, and it paid massive dividends for us.

In our sixth year as a company, Microsoft became a new market entrant in our industry. Having competed against and worked with Microsoft earlier in my career, I knew they would eventually dominate the market, so I forced our company to go "all in" on them early on. However, I received a ton of pushback from my internal teams. They all said that the Microsoft products were not market-ready yet (they weren't), that we didn't know anything about their products (we didn't), and that this was a considerable risk (sure, but I also knew the potential reward was massive). Despite the unclear outcome and minimal support, I pushed us full steam ahead. Our relationship with Microsoft and our offerings around their products became THE REASON why we were acquired for millions of dollars just a few short years later. To this day, as of the writing of this book, services around Microsoft encompass about ninety percent of the company's overall revenue. I later wondered what would have happened if we didn't react to the market. It surely wouldn't have been as happy of an ending. Adapt or die.

Ambitious: In the immortal words of the G.O.A.T. and my personal hero, Michael Jordan, "You must expect great things of yourself before you can do them." I love this quote. I think many people will tell you they are ambitious and that they want to be great. But first, you must believe in yourself before you go out to achieve great things. Since you are reading this book and considering starting your own business, I am guessing it is because you have already had success or believe you are capable of great things. I am here to tell you that you are right. Don't ever lose that. I instilled in my team that the company would always be ambitious, and I wanted ambitious people who wanted to be great on our team.

Entrepreneurial: This one was simple, and because of our origins of starting from scratch, this was already part of our DNA. I wanted people and hired people who liked being their own boss and wanted to take control of their life and career. We used to talk all the time about wanting self-motivated people who treated the business like their own and had the freedom to innovate.

Always Evolving and Never Sitting Idle: These were essentially the action items from being market-driven. But it was important for those at the company to know that we would never be stale.

It's Not Always Easy, But You Won't Ever Be Bored: Reid Hoffman once said, "Starting a company is like jumping out of an airplane and assembling the parachute on the way down." I agree. For a new business and startup, things move a million miles per hour. While this pace can be exciting, it can also be exhausting and frustrating. In the early days, it is unrealistic for all the company's internal operations to run smoothly.

My team often complained about not having all the resources a large company had. Additionally, they would get frustrated that we would be creating things from scratch, and many times, it fell on their shoulders to do it. I used to tell people, "There is no calvary coming; we are the calvary." However, it is important to be honest about the downsides of a startup. We acknowledged that we understood many things were more challenging at our company because we did not have all the resources and processes that more established organizations did. It didn't make anyone feel better about the situation, but at least they understood that we understood.

At the same time, this kind of crazy existence also attracted folks to us. Often, we would find people who had been stuck at a large Fortune 500 company for years and were sick of the routine and mundane nature of their existence. They were essentially bored. We used to joke with these folks that if they wanted crazy, we would be their huckleberry! Going back to the positive mindset lessons from earlier, it was "good" that things were hectic.

LEADERSHIP TEAM CHARACTERISTICS

After establishing and documenting the company's characteristics, I felt it was important to set expectations of what our employees could expect from the leadership team. Similarly, I documented and presented what that was. Here is what it looked like.

The Culture of Controle

- What can you expect of the Executive team:
    - To provide you opportunity
    - To create a Healthy Positive Working environment
    - For you to be rewarded professionally and financially for what you earn/deserve (not who you know or how long you have been here)
    - To give you freedom in your job
    - To give you the tools to be successful in your job
    - To knock down the roadblocks in your way and have your back
    - To make you proud to work at Controle
    - To continue to SUCCEED
    - Relentless pursuit of GREATNESS

I won't go through all of these in detail as most of them should be self-explanatory, but I will highlight and expand on a few and the reasoning behind the statement.

To Provide You Opportunity: One thing that became abundantly clear to me early in starting the business is that high-level performers want to have the ability to prove themselves. We became quite successful at recruiting talented people at other companies who felt they never had the opportunity to prove themselves or didn't get the opportunity for the job they wanted for whatever reason. These are the exact people you want to hire. I found that once you give them the opportunity they always wanted, they will run through walls for you and likely will succeed, as if for no other reason than they don't want to disappoint themselves and prove the naysayers right.

For You to Be Rewarded Professionally and Financially for What You Earn/Deserve (Not Who You Know or How Long You Have Been Here): To me, life has three certainties: death, taxes, and employees always wanting more money. You will never escape the jaws of employees wanting more and more money. I knew this would always be the case, and like any good salesperson, I brought up the objection proactively and discussed this openly in company meetings.

I made it simple for them. I used to tell my team, "You want more money? Great, bring more money in. It's that simple." For salespeople, this was self-explanatory. The more they sold, the more money they made. But for everyone else, they were on a salary-plus-bonus structure. They had quarterly bonuses based on their personal performance. I used to tell the people on salary and bonus structures that they would not all be treated equally. If we had a customer that always re-upped on our annual managed service because they loved the engineer ... Well, guess what? That engineer would make more money than one who wasn't helping bring in new business or helping keep existing business. This has the added benefit of creating a positive flywheel effect. I told my engineers that if customers were happy and re-upped because of them, they would get paid more. Therefore, they would give our customers the best customer experience, which made them more willing to re-up on the service. It's a win-win-win for everyone. So, incentivize your non-commissioned employees to help bring in or keep business, and everyone will be rewarded.

To Make You Proud to Work at Controle: Everyone wants to be associated with a winner. When you recruit people to come in and work for you, especially in the first few years, they will have a lot of anxiety about working for a small and unproven company. I even spoke to many spouses of prospective employees as they wanted to know why their husband or wife was leaving a "stable" job for this unknown startup with a weird E at the end of its company name. *Wait, are they Spanish-speaking or something?* I took a lot of pride in what we were trying to achieve and told this to the spouses. My goal was for anyone who ever came to work for my company to be proud that they worked there. The best way for them to be proud is to provide a healthy work environment, act with integrity, and become a success story. Aim for these same goals, and they will be proud that they were a part of it, as they should be.

Good is the Enemy of Great

- What separates Good from Great:
  - Not a strategy, a well defined strategy
  - Focus not only on what to do, but what not to do
  - Greatness was not a matter of destiny, it is a matter of conscious choice
  - Don't wait for people to change, act right away
  - Great companies allow people to be heard rather than dictated to
  - Better to have a strong team than one genius with 1000 helpers
  - Confront the brutal facts
  - Focus on a few things (or one thing) that we can do better than anyone else
  - Create a culture of discipline with an ethic of entrepreneurship

Relentless Pursuit of Greatness: Early on in building the company, I read the book *Good to Great* by Jim Collins, which is a fantastic book I highly recommend. This book studied companies in the same industry that had the same opportunity, looked at the differences between companies that had success, and compared it to others that had what would be categorized as great or significantly much more success. I wanted my company to be great. I had no interest in just being good. Good was for second place. Fuck second place—I wanted to be on top of the podium. I made the teachings of this book an instrumental part of our culture. At the beginning of every year, I had us revisit where we were at with meeting the goals of what a great company looks like. I gave an honest assessment with no BS. I would say, "Here is what that looked like," and score us on each bullet point with either a check mark for being on target or an X for not meeting the objective.

Once again, the point of this whole exercise is for your team to understand what you are going for and what you stand for. Then, going forward, when you make day-to-day decisions, you won't have to explain them, as the folks inside already know the company's core principles.

EMPLOYEE CHARACTERISTICS

For the last component of our company culture presentation and definition, I wrote down what the leadership team expected in return from our employees. This is what it looked like.

The Culture of Controle   CONTROL☺

- What Executive team expects of you:
    - Clients come first all day every day, that is who we ARE
    - Be a team player, there is no I it is We

    - Hold yourself accountable otherwise we will
    - Don't complain, suggest
    - Be honest/transparent and <u>over communicate</u>
    - Help us find A Players to add to our team
    - Your actions reflect the company as much as yourself, treat others with respect and put yourselves in others shoes
    - And as always remember our company motto: <u>JUST CARE</u>

***Random Side Note**: If you don't recognize the picture in the slide, it's a scene from the movie *Office Space*, one of my favorite movies and a huge fan favorite for many of our team as well. We officially adopted *Office Space* as our movie mascot. We constantly had pictures of scenes from it in our internal presentations. When we finally got a proper office space, we had two conference rooms. When I asked everyone what we should name them, Initech and Initrode, the two fictional companies from *Office Space*, won the day. Also, one of my favorite stories of something happening in our office is that being the jackass I am, I hung a picture of Bill Lumburg (see below) in our kitchen right above the coffee machine as a joke about people getting back to work. One day, a repairman was working in the kitchen, and he noticed the picture while my assistant Chrissy was helping him. He said, "So, what is this? Is that like your boss or something? He seems like a real asshole." Hilarity. The point of this whole random story is it's a good idea to bring humor into the workplace. It always makes the workplace more fun and helps relieve tensions when you don't take yourself too seriously. Life is serious enough.

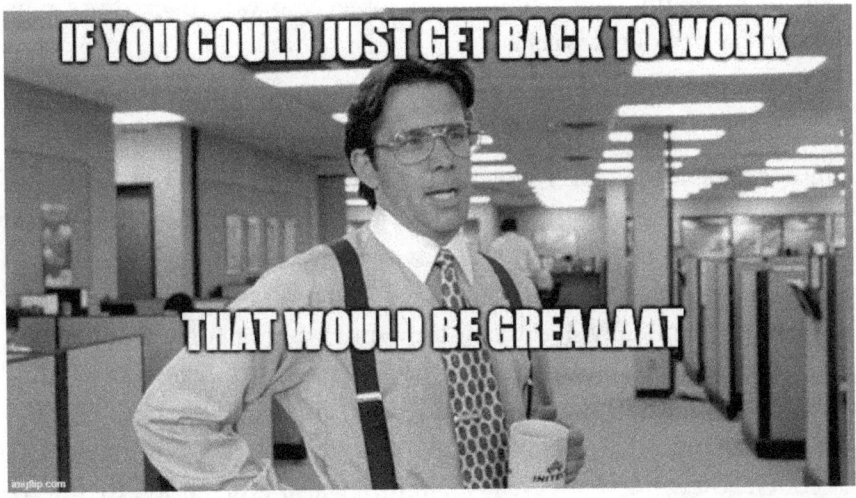

Ok, snap out of it, Kevvie. These people are busy and got shit to do. Get back to business and focus.

As before, I will not break down all of these items, as most are self-explanatory, but I will highlight a few.

Clients Come First All Day Every Day, That Is Who We ARE: This one is self-explanatory, but once again, right on the top is about being customer-focused. No one at my company could ever doubt our relentless focus on the customer when it was at the top of every list.

Hold Yourself Accountable; Otherwise, We Will: I always looked to hire self-motivated go-getters. When I interviewed people, I used to tell everyone that if we had to manage them, we would manage them out of the business. We didn't want followers; we wanted leaders. Leaders hold themselves accountable, so you don't have to. Look for leaders.

Don't Complain, Suggest: I used to hear complaints all the time. And, of course, people had every right to complain; as we just discussed, things are chaotic when you are in a startup. I eventually learned not to get too upset at complaints, as they mostly come from people caring and wanting things to be better. There is nothing wrong with that. It is healthy, and I will take people who care over those who don't every day of the week.

I used to tell people, "Don't tell me what you think I want to hear; tell me what you really think." Then the truth comes out, and it's usually some sort of complaint. I would then say, "Ok, great. What should we do about it, or how would we make it better?" Initially, this would typically stump people as it was not what they expected me to say. I would recognize this confusion and add, "It's ok; think about it and let me know." Eventually, I got it to the point where people would come and complain about something but would do it calmly and know they needed to suggest how we should do it differently. Many times, I would then put them in charge of coming up with the solution, which, of course, they didn't always love, but they also understood they were the right person for it. This approach can significantly open communication within the company, have people react way less emotionally, and come up with creative and usually practical solutions to the challenge. That's a win-win-win.

And As Always, Remember Our Company Motto: Just Care: For me, this was at the core of everything the company stood for. My whole career, when I was at various Fortune 500 companies, I saw so many employees who didn't give a shit. They didn't care about others they worked with. They didn't care about the customer. They didn't care about the effort they were putting into their job. They didn't care that their laziness negatively affected the rest of us. These people drove me fucking insane, and I avoided them like the plague where I could. I wanted people that cared as much about the customer and took pride in what they were doing as much as I did. I even had the company motto inscribed in our kitchen to remind people what we were all about.

After discovering that this was our company motto, I can't tell you how many customers told me how much they loved it and wished their company had something similar. Because everyone has worked with that one person or group who didn't care about their job, and it affected everyone around them. Our customers loved that we were a group that cared about their success and each other, resulting in our success.

To summarize, when defining company culture, go through an exercise and identify a) what you want it to be and b) what it already is. Then, write it down, communicate it to your team, and look for any refinement as you go on. Going forward, quarterly or annually, check in on where you are with the goals you set out for yourself, and be honest. Once you get this all dialed in and understood, culture can help you scale and become a competitive advantage, as customers and potential employees will gravitate to you if they can identify with it.

In conclusion, company culture is the silent force behind the scenes, shaping your team's and customers' experiences, guiding decisions, and fostering an environment of growth. This force distinguishes your business, not just as a place of work but as a community with a shared purpose and vision. Force defines your squad. So, "Use the Force, Luke."

#controleway

CHAPTER 17
BRANDING MASTERY—CRAFTING YOUR BUSINESS IDENTITY

> *Your brand is what other people say about you when you're not in the room.*
>
> JEFF BEZOS

Everyone has heard the term "brand" before. Not only do companies work hard to build their perception in the industry they serve, but in this digital age, branding has extended to individuals trying to carve out their own niche in a sea of social influencers. But do we really understand what branding is and the individual components that make up a brand? Let's break it down.

At its core, branding is the process of creating and managing the unique identity and perception of your business, product, or service in the minds of your customers. Crafting a brand encompasses many elements, including the name, logo, design, messaging, and overall customer experience working with your company. Effective branding helps distinguish your business from competitors, builds customer loyalty, and creates a lasting impression.

The first step in crafting a message around what you want customers to say about you when you are not in the room is to think about what makes you, you. What do you stand for? How would you like customers to think of you versus how they feel about your competition? Our efforts from crafting company culture in the previous chapter should funnel directly into our branding strategy.

Your branding efforts should clearly distinguish you from everyone else. If customers are faced with picking your company versus your competition for the same product or service, you want them to think, "Well, I am going to go with x product or company because of y." The "y" in this scenario is your brand.

Branding was a bit foreign to me when I first started the company, and I don't consider myself a branding guru by any means. In the first year, I didn't give it much thought beyond creating the company logo and our first few product names. A few years in, I decided to put more effort into it, which directly correlated with building the second version of our website. As I knew I needed help, I hired an outside branding consulting company to help me with the process, and they led our efforts in this space.

Before our engagement started, I read a few branding books to familiarize myself with the process and be more educated before we began. One of the exercises I found helpful was thinking about a brand you are personally loyal to and then reverse engineering how they got you to be a loyalist. The book argued that this would give you a better sense of how it works and, in turn, learn how to craft your own brand. So, I looked at a brand I was loyal to: Apple.

I love Apple products and services. I have an iPhone as my smartphone and an Apple Watch as my smartwatch. I subscribe to Apple One, and I use AirTags to track where my wallet and keys are. At this point, it would take a lot for me to switch from any of these products and services. But I wasn't always this "all in on Apple way," and I was late to the party. I used to have a Droid phone, a Fitbit for my fitness tracking, Napster for music streaming, and a Tile for item tracking.

The challenge with these products is that I consistently had technical issues with all of them. And in general, I am an impatient prick. My first foray into the Apple world was the iPhone. As mentioned, I previously had a Droid phone, but I had all sorts of issues with calls dropping and apps not working or being unavailable on the platform.

I was fed up and switched to the iPhone, and all those technical issues evaporated overnight. I have never looked back. I have had an iPhone for over a decade, and I am sitting here trying to think about how many times I have had problems with it. I am having a hard time thinking of a time I had a serious issue that rebooting didn't fix. It just works.

This technical excellence is why I switched from all the other devices and apps. My Fitbit had issues syncing, and it seemed like it broke every eighteen months. My kids constantly complained about using Napster and how it gave them issues. My Tile seemed to work half the time, which was ridiculously frustrating as the whole purpose of the device is to work when you are in a rush to find your keys or wallet. Over time, I switched to all the Apple products mentioned above, and guess what? My kids shut the hell up (well, at least about that issue). My AirTags always work and are way more accurate on location than the Tile. My Apple Watch is always synced and working and has the added bonus of way more features.

This is why I am loyal to Apple and will overpay for their products. Because their products JUST WORK. Whenever they come out with a new product in a category I am frustrated with, I don't even think about it, I just switch to them. That's an incredibly valuable brand they have built. It may mean something different to you, but for me, the Apple brand stands for consistency and technical excellence. I don't have to worry if their products will work—they just do, so I am incredibly loyal to them. That is what I say about Apple when they are not in the room. Wait, are they in the room right now? Siri?

Now that we have discussed the ideology of building the brand, let's break it down and look at the individual building blocks. Building the brand from scratch incorporates several items. Let's look at them now, using Apple as an example company. Because, really, how in the world did they make so many of us such rabid fans?

BRAND NAME

This could be a company, product, or service name. Apple is the overarching brand name. Still, a whole brand exists around their other products and services, such as the iPhone (product) and Apple Music (service).

The key to the brand name is to make it easy to remember and pronounce. When the first iPhone came out, I didn't need to think about what it was; I knew what it was. Additionally, you want to make it meaningful to its intended target audience. Early on, Apple had an "I" in front of its products, such as the iPod, iPad, and iPhone. This "i" signified to its target audience of young technology-friendly customers that it was a digital product and part of the new move to "internet-connected devices," which is hilarious to think about as a feature as we write this in 2024.

BRAND IDENTITY

This is the visual element of your brand and is made up of several items.

- **Logo**: A logo is a visual symbol that represents the brand and is easily recognizable. For Apple, this is the apple with the bite taken out of it. I know you can picture it in your brain right now. There is no mistaking it.
- **Color Scheme**: These are consistent colors that evoke specific emotions and align with the brand's personality. Apple uses a lot of white in its branding. White represents purity, simplicity, and cleanliness. It is often used by brands that want to convey a minimalist, modern, and straightforward image. Apple uses white to highlight its clean, simple, and user-friendly design.
- **Typography**: Typography encompasses fonts that reflect the tone and style of the brand. Apple uses many lowercase typography and a modern font in their products. Modern fonts typically feature clean lines and a minimalist design.

They convey a sense of forward-thinking and sophistication, making them ideal for brands in technology, fashion, and high-end products. These fonts often suggest innovation and elegance.
- **Imagery**: Imagery is made up of visual elements such as photos, graphics, and videos that convey the brand's message. Apple has always stood out for its ability to have cool-looking ads with straightforward messages. Further, they use images of young and healthy-looking models, the type of people we all want to look like. So, if you buy an Apple product, you can be young and beautiful, too!

BRAND VOICE AND TONE

Brand voice and tone are how a brand speaks to its intended audience. Ensuring this voice and tone are carried throughout all your customers' touchpoints is critical.

- **Voice**: Brand voice is a consistent expression of the brand through words, style, and tone. Apple's communications are straightforward and clear. Instead of saying that their iPod was an electronic device with a hard drive containing digital music files you could play on demand, Apple said it was "1,000 songs in your pocket."
- **Tone**: Apple's tone speaks to its customers in a relatable and human manner. They consistently use the words "you" and "your" to be more engaging to us all.

BRAND MESSAGE

A brand message is what companies use to convey what they are all about and how they stand apart from their competition; it has several different components.

- **Tagline**: This is a short, memorable phrase that captures the brand's essence. Apple's is "Think Different."

- **Mission Statement**: This is a concise statement that defines the brand's purpose and what it aims to achieve. Apple's is "To bring the best user experience to its customers through its innovative hardware, software, and services."
- **Value Proposition**: This is a clear articulation of the brand's benefits and value to its customers. Apple's is "Innovative products that enhance your life."

BRAND EXPERIENCE

Brand experience is how consumers will engage directly with your team and products, and it has a few different components.

- **Customer Service**: This is the quality of interaction and service provided to customers. Apple was a pioneer in bringing a tech company's customer service into a brick-and-mortar store. Their "Genius Bar" allows you to walk into any Apple store and meet with a person face to face to discuss and solve any issues you have with their products. I have always found the folks working in these Genius Bars helpful, knowledgeable, and friendly. I am more loyal to Apple than their competitors, knowing that if I have problems with one of their products, I can drive ten miles and talk to a real-life person to help me resolve it.
- **User Experience**: This is the overall experience of customers when they interact with your brand, including website usability, product packaging, and in-store experience. Apple is the granddaddy master of user experience, like nothing we have ever seen. Everyone knows what opening one of your first Apple products felt like. The packaging was ridiculously well done and thought out, like something I had never seen before. It's an experience in itself. I remember thinking, man, if they spent this much time thinking about packaging, think about how much time they must have thought about the product. As the saying goes, "How you do one thing is how you do everything." Additionally, their website is straightforward to use and has a beautiful design. Finally, my

mind was absolutely blown when my two-year-old picked up an iPad and figured out how to use it on his own without anyone telling him. That is fucking mind-blowing user experience design, and from someone who has attempted to do it before, it's truly breathtaking.

BRAND VALUES

Brand values are the core principles and beliefs that guide a brand's behavior and decision-making. Yes, for-profit companies have a conscience, too. I mean, of course, they do. Right? Well, we are *homo sapiens*, after all, so we do our best. Brand values consist of a few different parts.

- **Core Principles:** These are the fundamental beliefs and values that guide a brand's actions and decisions. Apple's core principles have always been innovation, quality, design, and user experience.
- **Cultural Relevance**: The alignment of the brand's values with its target audience's cultural and social values. Apple's cultural relevance has historically been about environmental responsibility and individual empowerment to provide tools that enhance individual creativity, productivity, innovation, and social responsibility, reflecting the characteristics of their desired audience.

Now that we have deconstructed Apple's brilliant branding, I will relay some of my company's actions and thoughts behind them. And no, I don't claim we were anywhere near Apple. No one is. But just because this is what we did, it is not necessarily what you should do. As mentioned, branding is all about looking internally at yourself and then screaming from the rooftops what that is. Let's briefly look at what we did at Controle and the reasons why to help you on your way for the rest of us non-Apple branding mortals.

BRAND NAME

As mentioned, I handled our branding efforts in the first two years. As you know, I came up with the company name Controle based on the efforts we talked about in Chapter 6. Further, I came up with our Bridge the Gap service name from a conversation I had with a customer, which we talked about in Chapter 13.

When I sat down with the company I hired to help us with branding, I explained the significance of the name Controle. He particularly liked the "e" at the end of the name and liked that it was sideways, as it stood out and was different. He suggested incorporating that "e" into as many product and service names as possible. We took his lead for the two software products we created: They were called eGovern, which was a tool that helped customers electronically govern their data, and eNotify, which was a tool that helped customers electronically notify their employees that their data was going to be included in a lawsuit. We carried the crooked E from our logo, but this time, we mixed it up and put it at the beginning of the word instead of the end. For our customers, it was unmistakable that these were our products.

Here is what those looked like:

BRAND IDENTITY

Let's examine some of the elements of the brand identity I developed and why.

Logo

As discussed earlier in the book, I used 99designs to help create our company logo. As I went through the process, I learned more about what specific colors and fonts in your logo could help portray to your intended audience. It's pretty fascinating. Below, I will break down what I chose. In the appendix at the end of this book, I have added the other colors and some other fonts and explained what they mean.

Color Scheme

For the color scheme, I chose blue as the color. Blue conveys a sense of trust, reliability, and professionalism. It is calming and often used by brands that want to be seen as dependable and trustworthy. For example, IBM and my buddies at Microsoft use blue to communicate reliability and professionalism. For us, it was essential to portray trust and reliability. We were dealing with sensitive issues for our customers, and they needed someone who knew what they were doing and could be relied on in an emergency. So blue was an easy choice.

Additionally, I wanted the "e" in our logo to stand out and be different from the rest of the letters so customers could know it stood for electronic data. So, I made the "e" crooked. For the color, I chose green because a) I wanted it to stand out, and B) the color green portrays tranquility. Our customers were dealing with highly stressful situations, and I wanted them to look at us as a calming influence to work with.

Typography

Then it came down to figuring out what to do for the logo's typography, another fascinating space. This comes down to the fonts you will use and what those fonts will say about your business. In the appendix are some examples of other fonts, but I went with a modern font, Avant Garde.

Let's take a look at modern fonts and what they convey. Examples are Avant Garde, Century Gothic, and Montserrat, and their attributes are generally futuristic, stylish, and sophisticated. Modern fonts typically feature clean lines and a minimalist design. They convey a sense of forward-thinking and sophistication, making them ideal for brands in technology, fashion, and high-end products. As discussed earlier, our friends at Apple use a modern sans-serif font to emphasize innovation, simplicity, and elegance.

We used a sans-serif font, ITC Avant Garde Gothic, specifically the bold version. I wanted a no-nonsense, simple font that portrayed professionalism, trustworthiness, and straightforwardness. As you have already seen, here is what the result looked like. For a color version of it, go online and Google image Controle logo. I loved it then and still do now.

You might see some consistency in my choices. Did you notice the color and typeface of the title on the cover of this book? Yep, I wanted to project trust, stability, and strength. Ask yourself if it aided in your decision to buy this book.

Imagery

Imagery is made of visual elements such as photos, graphics, and videos that convey the brand's message.

In our first meeting with the outsourced branding company, they asked me to explain the business issue we were solving. I told them it was a terrifying issue for our customers. I won't get into the nitty gritty, but essentially, there are all sorts of best practices and rules around preserving and producing electronic data associated with lawsuits and investigations. It's serious business. If people did it the wrong way or, worse, did something bad on purpose, they could put their company in a terrible spot and, in the case of extreme situations, personally face jail time if they did something nefarious. So, they were scared shitless of doing it wrong. I relayed a true story to the branding company about how one time, a customer of mine was so terrified that he fucked up that he started crying in front of me out of the fear he was going to jail. And this was just him doing his job. The branding company feverishly wrote notes down.

Additionally, as we talked, I told the branding company that I liked to be different, and I wanted our website and marketing materials to be different from all the other companies in our industry. Our competitors' websites and marketing material were stale, serious, and boring. And that made sense, as we were all selling to attorneys at large corporations. When people think of attorneys in general, they think of serious people. So, I get it; it made sense to market that way.

But luckily for Kevvie, I knew something they didn't know. I knew, having been raised by an attorney and around them all my life, that behind the pomp and circumstance, they were fun-loving and, in general, surprisingly, had a really good sense of humor. I guess you had to develop a sense of humor when dealing with serious shit all day long. So, I knew there was a real opportunity to stand out in the crowd by making our website and marketing fun. Additionally, that went along with who we were as a company. We were different. We were more fun than the other companies, so why not roll with it?

I told the marketing company about this and let them do their thing. A month later, they returned to my office and presented their thoughts. They presented what essentially was a cartoon video that walked the viewer through the problem that we solved. Early in the video, it said, "Controlling data is scary... scary like a yeti!" and then a yeti burst through the screen. Further, the rest of the commercial had the yeti popping up, putting out fires, and driving a car. I thought to myself, "What the hell is this? What am I watching? I don't know how professional this is, but I love it!" I laughed out loud, and the hairs stood on my arm. I knew it was goofy, but I also knew it would stand out. I showed it to some of the team in the office, and they were all laughing and said we had to do it. We then decided to show some of our best customers, including a few that I felt were more serious. I will not lie; I was a bit reluctant to do so. To my surprise, they also all loved it, unanimously. So, I said fuck it, not only are we going to greenlight the yeti, let's go all in on the yeti.

Here is a link to the video: https://bit.ly/Yottabyte

Not only did we include the Yeti in almost everything, we even gave him a name: Yottabyte. A yottabyte (YB) is a unit of digital information storage that represents 1,000,000,000,000,000,000,000,000 bytes. We thought this name was clever since we were helping our customers manage electronic information. Get it, Yottabyte the Yeti? I created that one on my own in one of my TM sessions. *Nice work, Kevvie! Hey, thanks, guy.*

Further, the Yottabyte commercials were a huge hit with my kids. When people asked them what my company did (they were little), they would say, "He has Yetis in his commercials!" They loved Yottabyte. For Father's Day, they bought me a yeti statue, and it sat in our office at Controle and now in my home office (see pic below). Further, I have received more yeti gifts (socks, t-shirts, hats, and stickers) than I can count. Never in a million years did I think that Yetis would become such a big part of my life when I started the company. It's another weird and awesome path your life can take when you create your own adventure. I love it.

From then on, most of our website and marketing imagery had the same cartoonish feel and the yeti in it. Was it weird? Sure. Was it a bit amateurish? Maybe. Was it effective? You bet your ass. I can remember one of the first times I was introduced to the top analyst at Gartner in our space, someone who we needed to impress so he would give our products a good review. One of the first things he said to me was, "Aren't you the yeti guys?" I sheepishly said, "Um… yeah," thinking he was about to blast me for being amateur. He continued, "I am not going to lie; the first time I saw it, I thought it was ridiculous and unprofessional. But then it grew on me, and now I think of you guys all of the time because of that yeti." Spoiler alert: he referred us to a lot of potential customers and gave our products a good review. Was that because of the yeti? I'm not sure, but it certainly didn't hurt us.

BRAND VOICE AND TONE

We adopted a more casual, laid-back voice throughout our messaging to put our customers at ease as they dealt with stressful situations. Otherwise, just like Apple, we used words like "you and your" to make it relatable and convey to our customers that we were thinking about them and not ourselves. Also, ask yourself, are YOU seeing a trend here with my decisions on voice?

BRAND MESSAGE

As you can see at the end of the commercial, our brand messaging and tagline was "Mitigate risk. Reduce Costs. Take Controle." Our customers only cared about two things when working with us: reducing the risks of collecting and preserving this data or saving money on their current or future processes. They always did business with us for one of these two reasons, so we just threw them in our tagline.

BRAND EXPERIENCE

As we discussed in the customer-centric and culture chapters, I always instilled that our customers came first all day, and we take care of them at any cost. We always strived to provide the best customer service, and we were successful at it. We were recognized by both EMC and Microsoft Corporation and won awards for our customer service and satisfaction. We always looked to give our customers amazing service, which is why they returned to us. "Controle always takes care of my problem no matter what" is what we wanted our customers to say about us when we weren't in the room.

Further, we always strived to make the interfaces as easy-to-use as possible for the software products we created. I routinely used my two-year-old son's iPad experience example as a goal. Not to say that we ever got there, but we strived to make our products as easy-to-use as possible so people didn't have to waste mental cycles on them.

BRAND VALUES

You already know that our principles revolved around being focused on the customer and market-driven. Further, internally, we always talked about empowering our employees to take control of their lives. I loved that many of our employees took advantage of this and would move somewhere they always wanted to and work remotely for months on end, and they didn't need permission from us to do so. I even followed their lead and did the same with my family. Further, we worked to give back to the community. Every year, we give the team an extra day off to do service work. Afterward, we had them report back to the company on what they had done and present it to everyone on a Monday morning meeting. Further, whenever we had company in-person get-togethers, one of the days had a service day included in it. So, make sure you find ways to identify your values and then show them in action.

In conclusion, branding is an intricate process that you must think through. First, think about what you stand for and what makes you unique. This is the backbone of what you want to guide all the decisions you must make for the individual components. Further, think through a brand you are loyal to and how to do something similar. Then, break down the building blocks and remain consistent in your messaging. Now that we have looked at building our brand, we will take our company and our products to the streets! Marketing, here we come.

CHAPTER 18
INBOUND AND OUT OF BOUNDS—EFFECTIVE MARKETING FOR THE NEW BUSINESS

> *If you have more money than brains, you should focus on outbound marketing. If you have more brains than money, you should focus on inbound marketing.*
>
> GUY KAWASAKI, VENTURE CAPITALIST AND AUTHOR

Now that we have done all the work to identify our customers' problems and create solutions, how do we find and speak to the people who want to buy them? This is where marketing comes into play. Marketing in itself is a broad subject. However, I always considered marketing to be the effort we make to find prospective customers.

Before we start, let's look at the traditional definition of marketing. Marketing is the strategic process of creating, communicating, delivering, and exchanging offerings that have value for customers. It encompasses various activities, including market research, product development, pricing strategies, distribution channels, advertising, and sales. As we have covered many of these bespoke items already and will talk about sales next, what I decided to do for this specific chapter is to look at the two main different methods, inbound and outbound marketing, look at the pros and cons of each, share my personal experiences, and specifically look at it through the lens of practical methods for the new or young company.

In essence, outbound marketing is when you contact people to find opportunities, and inbound marketing is what you do to have people contact you. You want people to contact you. Let's look at the components of both now.

OUTBOUND MARKETING

Outbound marketing, or "traditional marketing," refers to the strategies and tactics where businesses initiate the conversation by pushing their message out to a wide audience. This approach aims to reach potential customers through various forms of proactive outreach. All these methods have been used on you, and as we go through them, think about how effective they were in leading you to purchase something.

Let's take a look at the standard methods of outbound marketing.

1. Outbound marketing **advertising** methods include TV and radio commercials, print ads (newspapers, magazines), and online ads (banner ads, pop-ups).
2. **Direct mail** involves sending promotional materials like catalogs, brochures, postcards, and letters to your potential customers' mailboxes. Then they go through the mail and say, "Huh, what is this?" and throw it directly in the trash can.
3. **Telemarketing and cold calling** involve making unsolicited phone calls to potential customers to promote products or services. If you are lucky, they pick up the phone, but then they swear at you and hang up. Party!
4. **Email marketing** in outbound marketing involves sending unsolicited promotional emails to a list of potential or existing customers. If not targeted and permission-based, this is often considered spam. Customers then open your email, unsubscribe, delete it, and curse your name for wasting their time.

5. **Trade shows and events** are where you participate in or sponsor events where you can showcase your products and services to a large audience. We found this to be a relatively effective approach but expensive and time-consuming.
6. **Billboards and outdoor advertising** involve using large outdoor displays and signs to capture the attention of people driving by. Regrettably, there were no Yottabyte billboards for your viewing pleasure.

The challenges around outbound marketing are apparent. First, it can be expensive due to the high costs of print or online advertising campaigns, production of materials, and distribution, including hard and soft costs (the time spent by those doing telemarketing, for example). Further, it's less targeted, which will lead to you reaching out to a ton of people who could give two shits. Finally, it's intrusive; as my kids say, outbound marketing is like a "try-hard"—a kid constantly annoying you and trying too hard to impress, but you couldn't care less. Don't be a try-hard, bruh.

On the flip side, outbound marketing has some value: It effectively reaches a large and diverse audience. Also, it often generates quick responses for leads, especially for time-sensitive promotions. Finally, it is effective for brand awareness, i.e., getting your name out there on a grand scale.

In summary, while outbound marketing remains a viable strategy for businesses, especially for building brand awareness and reaching a broad audience, it is much more practical for large, established companies with significant cash coffers. As that is likely not your situation, let's focus on what inbound marketing is and why it makes way more sense for a startup.

INBOUND MARKETING

Inbound marketing is a strategy focusing on attracting customers by creating valuable content and experiences tailored to them. Unlike outbound marketing, which involves pushing messages out, inbound marketing aims to draw people in. Here are the key elements and principles of inbound marketing:

1. **Content Creation and Distribution**: Inbound marketing emphasizes creating valuable, relevant, and consistent content that attracts and engages your target audience. Content can include blog posts, articles, in-person presentations, videos, infographics, podcasts, eBooks, and more.
2. **SEO (Search Engine Optimization)**: We all know how beneficial it is to appear on the top of the first page of search tools like Google. Inbound marketing emphasizes optimizing your website's content to rank higher in these search engine results pages (SERPs), so potential customers can easily find you.
3. **Social Media Marketing:** This involves using social media platforms to share content, engage with your audience, and build a community around your brand.
4. **Lead Generation:** In inbound marketing, lead generation moves away from reaching out and toward capturing leads through various means, such as presentations to partners, forms on your website, gated content, and landing pages. Call-to-actions (CTAs) can guide visitors toward specific actions, like signing up for a newsletter or downloading a resource.
5. **Email Marketing:** Email marketing is very different in inbound marketing than outbound marketing. Instead of spamming people, you nurture relationships with your leads and customers by sending them personalized and relevant email content.

There are many advantages to inbound marketing for a new or young company. First, it is much more cost-effective and practical, focusing on organic traffic and content creation, which you can control. Additionally, it is much more targeted instead of yelling into the crowd. It attracts visitors actively seeking information about your products or services, leading to higher-quality leads. And trust me, low-quality leads are worse than no leads at all, as they are an incredible time suck. Inbound marketing also helps build trust and authority. Providing valuable content establishes your brand as an authority in your industry, building trust with your audience before they even talk to you. Finally, inbound marketing methods are much more customer-centric and focus on creating a positive experience for them, leading to higher satisfaction and loyalty.

So, what are the downsides? Unfortunately, it is more time-consuming. It does require significant time to create this quality content and time to build relationships. Further, it demands discipline and consistency. Success with inbound marketing depends on consistently producing and sharing valuable content and building relationships. Finally, it may take longer to see results than outbound marketing, as it involves building organic traffic and nurturing leads and relationships over time.

In summary, inbound marketing is about attracting the right audience, providing valuable content, and nurturing relationships to convert them into loyal customers. It is a sustainable, customer-focused approach that aligns with modern consumer behavior and our digital-first environment.

Now that we have examined the different strategies, I will walk you through some of the specific lessons we learned and some of the critical elements that will aid you in being successful in marketing.

INBOUND MARKETING THROUGH STRATEGIC PARTNERSHIPS

One area I'm uniquely qualified to discuss—and that you won't find much tactical advice on in other business books—is building a network of partners and empowering them to find deals for you. Your phone will ring off the hook as a result. I will walk you through it all now. But bear with me as I have to take you through how I figured it out.

Looking back, I am fortunate I had the first two sales jobs out of college that I did, as they taught me a ton about inbound and outbound marketing and their effectiveness. My first job was for Dell Computer Corporation, which at the time was one of the fastest-growing technology companies and stocks of all time. I loved my time at Dell. My job was to field inbound telephone calls, understand what the customer needed in a computer, walk them through the options, and try to get them to buy (a.k.a. close) on that first phone call. It was great; I didn't have to make many outbound calls or find deals on my own. All I had to do was wait for the phone to ring and do my thing. *Oh snap, I am a poet and know it.* I didn't have to worry about marketing as the Dell machine did it for me. This pure sales job with little responsibility for marketing is a salesperson's dream, but it is not typical.

My second job couldn't have been more different. I went to work for a small Microsoft consulting company that had little brand recognition, and the phone never rang. So now marketing was on my plate. For the first time, I had to figure out a way to find customers who may or may not want to buy our products and services. I learned quickly just how difficult and inefficient outbound marketing was. I used to sit in a room all day and cold-call people for eight hours. The amount of rejection was brutal. I would make somewhere from 100 to 200 calls per day, and it was a terrific day if I got one lead out of it. It was exhausting, inefficient, and demoralizing. Further, I would do email blasts and have similar dismal success rates. I couldn't find a solution that worked. I felt like I was bashing my head against a wall every day, and there was no solution. I had enough of the headache and left that job after less than a year.

Due to my experience with these two companies, I decided always to look to create what Dell did: to find a way to have customers call me instead of the other way around. It's just more efficient and effective. I took the lessons learned from those two jobs and worked to incorporate them into my next ones. I even picked companies where I felt inbound marketing was doable.

For my next sales job, I was at a copier company named IKON. It was a big company but typically did not receive many inbound calls, and if they did, they weren't going to newbie sales reps like me. I decided I had to find a way to get leads to come to me. This is where I learned the beauty of selling through partnerships.

At IKON, I started as a direct sales rep selling copier machines, but they quickly realized that because of my training and experience at Dell, I was a better fit for their software division. I was hired into that role six months in. In this role, I had to find my own leads, but I could also train the copier reps to find deals. They would bring me in, I'd help them close the sale, and we'd both get paid. I was an "overlay" or "sales specialist," as they call it, in technology sales. This is a common role where main-line sales reps will have someone who is an expert in a particular field or product. They can bring them in to help them sell, and both get paid. This is where I learned the value of partnering, and I honed my chomps in using it for inbound marketing, i.e., finding ways for people to call me with opportunities versus the other way around.

I decided I needed to crack the code to get these copier reps to find me deals. I talked to a number of my new peers about what they did. They spent most of their time trying to get these reps so educated that they would sell deals with little involvement from these specialists, and the specialists would look for their own deals in the meantime. Having been a copier rep, I knew there was no way they could figure it out on their own. They had many other distractions. Selling the software was much harder for them, and it represented a smaller portion of their overall revenue quota. My peers, not shockingly, weren't having much success with their approach and complained that I shouldn't expect many leads. But to me, it felt like there was something there, but I clearly needed to take a different approach than they had.

Instead of trying to turn these reps into experts in selling the software, I decided I wanted to train them solely on how to identify opportunities. I couldn't care less if they knew anything about selling the software. I viewed it as that wasn't their job; it was mine. I tailored my presentation to be what to look for in a customer, what to ask, and what to say to get another meeting where they could bring me in, and I would help them sell it. That was it. The presentation was ten minutes versus the hour-plus long, boring, overly technical sessions my peers were doing. Also, I did it all from their perspective of "WIIFM" or "What Is In It For Me?" I would teach them that all they had to do was ask a few questions and help find me a deal. Then, I would do everything for them; they didn't need to be involved and would still get paid. Free money. I made it a no-brainer for them.

This wound up being a successful model. My phone started ringing off the hook immediately. Right off the get-go, the amount of leads I got daily went up fivefold without much additional work. I could cast a much wider net without much personal effort. Then, I could also find my own deals and work on them. This double whammy led to me getting off to a fast start and turning heads from my peers on what I was doing.

Due to the approach's success, I decided to double down. At the time, we were reselling software products from other companies such as IBM and EMC Corporation. In particular, I had a lot of success with the EMC software, as I understood it well; it solved a clear customer problem and was easy to prove.

I also knew that whenever I resold one of the deals, somewhere, an EMC sales rep was getting paid and did zero work on the deal. It was free money to them. So, I thought, how can I get these EMC reps to do the same thing the IKON reps do? They could help find me deals, I would do all the work, and they would get paid. So, I cold-called the EMC regional sales leader, Tim Frank, and left a voicemail on his phone that gave a fifteen-second overview of what I wanted to do. I asked if he could spare ten minutes (and I specifically said that amount). In these ten minutes, I would walk him through the deals I had already closed for them and how we could do much more with minimal effort from his team. As he was swamped and these deals were a small percentage of his overall revenue, he reluctantly agreed to meet with me after some pestering. But he told me that I had to meet him at 6 am in his office and that he would give me at most ten minutes. *No problem.*

When I met with him, I gave him the overview and only focused on what was in it for him and his team, nothing about me or the software product. He was great. He agreed to make an introduction to his teams and for me to take it from there. For the next several weeks, I met with these EMC sales teams and took the same approach I did to train the IKON reps on "WIIFM" to work with me. Immediately after most meetings, the phone started ringing off the hook, and my sales increased even more. It got to the point where I had so much success selling deals and working with their teams that EMC recruited me to work for them about six months later. I got an offer to join them, one I couldn't refuse, and I wound up joining them. That job was the direct channel through which I started Controle, resulting in me selling the company and fulfilling all my wildest dreams. All this was accomplished by figuring out how to use partners to help you find deals.

Further, while building Controle, this is the same model I used: I would go to the EMC reps I used to work with and their newbies and train them to find deals and pass them on to me. Then, as we grew and I hired others, we used this same model with every other partner we worked with, and it was particularly effective and game-changing in our relationship with Microsoft. As I mentioned, Microsoft entered our industry about six years into my company. We were aggressive about getting in front of the Microsoft reps and giving them the same WIIFM training session. We told them we would help them sell their software, and we wanted the services. Our phone rang off the hook, and our Microsoft revenue doubled quarter over quarter for the next several years as a result. It's the number one reason why, a few years later, I had numerous companies reaching out to buy us, and one did. So yeah, working with partners for inbound marketing works like a dream.

So, my challenge for you is to think about companies out there whose customers would benefit from your product and service and whom you can compensate for making introductions to you and your team. Compensation can come in many forms, from helping drive revenue for their products (ideal) to sharing profits. Be creative. If you can build this stable of folks working on your behalf, your phone will ring off the hook, so get ready for the rocket ship ride of your life.

CONTENT MARKETING

Now, let's look at some other valuable lessons we learned, and we will start with **content marketing**. As part of the rebranding efforts you learned about in the last chapter, we updated most of our marketing materials. We focused primarily on developing content that we could put online. For simple content like blog posts or case studies, we made it readily available on our site. For more detailed content, such as whitepapers or presentations, we incorporated a "Call to Action" or CTA, meaning people had to provide their contact information to access it.

CTAs serve to understand who finds value in your content so you can reach out to them, and they are an effective and non-obtrusive way to build your email marketing list. Now, this doesn't mean that people won't put in fake information (Wow, who knew Johnny Appleseed was in the market for eDiscovery software or even was alive!) or that your competitors won't go on there and try to steal your content (they will), but it's still a good idea. Most of the time, the folks who enter their real information agree to speak further.

We focused on high-value content that didn't exist in other places or niche content surrounding new areas of developing technology or trends, and we knew people were seeking information from our market research efforts. The point is to get inside your customers' heads and create valuable content they will search for and then find you.

Another vital marketing component to highlight is leveraging **social proof**. In the brilliant book *Influence* by Robert Cialdini, which I highly recommend for any aspiring entrepreneur, he discusses the idea of social proof. Social proof is a psychological phenomenon that when people are unsure what to do, they will look to do what others have done and follow suit. Businesses understand this and use it to their advantage. Social proof can manifest in several ways: using experts or celebrities to endorse a product (hey, if the Kardashians use it, so should I!), user reviews and testimonials, social media shares and likes, and case studies and success stories, for example.

The significance of this social proof is precisely WHY I have so shamelessly asked for your review multiple times and why I created all the bonus content for you if you do! Yes, I know I am being a try-hard, but I also know that people are FAR more likely to buy this book if they see reviews of others before them.

The reason I am so obviously groveling for a review is that I decided that I wanted to self-produce this book so I would have creative control over the content. As mentioned, I am a control freak. However, I am a completely unknown author and don't have an outside publishing company helping market or pushing this book, so social proof via reviews are really what people will go off to buy this book or not. So please help a brotha out and take the time to give me a review! I wouldn't even be mad if you just dropped everything in your life and did it right now. Wait, you aren't going to? It's okay ... I will just wait. Just playing. But in all seriousness, I would really appreciate it. All you have to do is post a review and send me a screenshot or the link to the review to review@itstheblueprint.com. In the end of the book, you will see all the content you will receive for leaving the review. Thank you and I love you.

Ok, ok, ok! Uncle! We got it already. Are you done yet bruh? Ok fine back to the book.

For my company, leveraging the customer review method was more challenging as our customers were dealing with highly sensitive matters, and most did not want to discuss it publicly. But we did have some raving fans, and we created a whole section on our website where we had testimonials from some of our customers with names and quotes. One of our customers wanted to keep their name and organization private but allowed us to say that they were a Fortune 500 auto manufacturer. So even though no name was tied to it and it looked odd, their words still rang true. If your customer wants to be anonymous but is willing to give you a testimonial, take it. In the beginning, when you are unknown, you need all the social proof you can get.

Finally, regarding content marketing, we spent a lot of time creating case studies of customers who had successfully worked with us. We would document their problem, what we did to help them, and the results. These were frequently the most-read documents on our site and our created content that led to receiving the most leads.

EMAIL MARKETING

Let's also look at some valuable lessons we learned about **email marketing.** We went through our Salesforce system and created two types of "customers," and we tailored our content to these two different categories. One category was content we made for our customers with whom we were doing transactions. We also considered the sales folks and other people at our partners, like EMC and Microsoft, who were finding us leads as customers. Our messages to these two different customers were very different.

For the customers we transacted business with, we would do a monthly email marketing newsletter to summarize our blog posts for the month, provide links to them, and also offer Wall Street Journal and other online sources with interesting topics in our space. For our partners, we focused on new success stories that we had been a part of in hopes that they would say, "Oh wait, I also have a car manufacturer customer; maybe I should call them to learn more." More than anything, this was to stay at the top of the customer's minds and provide them with content specifically tailored to them and that we knew they would care about.

So, as you think about email marketing, don't just focus on those who are buying from you; think about those who are helping you get people to buy from you and market to them as well. Not many do, and you will stand out if you do.

SEO OPTIMIZATION OF OUR PAGE

SEO is fascinating. Still, it is also not something I pretend to be an expert in, and there are others whom you should listen to before me. However, from a high-level perspective, it makes sense to become further educated in this space and work with an expert to determine how to get your content on the first page of Google.

How to do this is highly nuanced, and as we learned in the IP section, Google has a trade secret on its algorithm, so this is not easily done. But if you are successful here, it's a phenomenal way to get customers to call you. We had a decent success rate in having people search organically and come to our site. But that was certainly aided by our niche market with targeted messaging.

In conclusion, every company must make an effort to find customers, and there are many ways to do so. However, inbound marketing is the preferred method for startups with limited budgets. By providing valuable content and forging strong relationships, your company can be primed for long-term success and a steady stream of customers knocking on your door.

CHAPTER 19
BUILDING THE SALES TEAM

> *EVERYONE is in sales. Everyone is selling something.*
>
> KEVIN BARNICLE, ME, THE AUTHOR OF THIS BOOK, FOUNDER/CEO OF CONTROLE, AND, AS YOU KNOW BY NOW, OVERALL SWELL GUY

Did this guy really just quote himself in his own book? Wasn't it enough that he already quoted Ace Ventura? Wow, what is this guy's deal? I have said this line so many times in my life that I had to include it. It is truly how I feel. Even if you are not in a direct sales role, you are selling something. Doctors and attorneys are selling their expertise to get you to work with them, not someone else. Financial advisors are selling that they can make you more money than others. Employees are constantly selling their boss that they deserve that promotion or more money. Everyone is selling their peers and themselves that they are up to the task. You are selling something, so stop pointing your nose down at salespeople.

But I understand because growing up, I also had a negative connotation of sales and salespeople. There are many folks out there that whenever they hear the term "salesperson," they think of some slimy used car salesman who is only out for him or herself. Because let's be honest, we have all encountered sleazy salespeople. For many of us, it happened at a young, impressionable age. I remember being so uncomfortable around car salespeople when my dad dragged me to the car dealership. It was very adversarial. After witnessing that, I never in a million years thought I would pursue a sales career.

But then, as a kid, I took my first sales job and immediately changed my opinion on the whole industry. Part of the responsibility of growing up in my household was that you HAD to have a job. My dad would not bend on this rule. At the time, I wouldn't say I liked it, but looking back, I am glad he did it for us, as my siblings and I all have a strong work ethic, more than most. The deal with my father was that we could pick out any job, but if we didn't find one or, as he affectionately referred to it, "took our sweet ass time doing so", he would pick one out for us and always would find the most difficult jobs he could find.

So, as fate would have it, as I was looking for a new job, I saw a sign on the side of the road that read, "Hiring! $20 per hour. No experience necessary." At the time, in the mid-1990s, $20 an hour was a ton of money. My previous job was working at a grocery store for a minimum wage of $4.25 an hour. And it's not like it was a fun job. I was busting my ass, pushing shopping carts around for hours in the scorching heat of Chicago summers. So, I thought that making five times the amount of money was worth whatever the hell I had to do.

The job was selling knives, specifically Cutco Knives. If you haven't heard of Cutco, it's a high-end cutlery product that has been around for three-fourths of a century and sells primarily through a direct selling approach of selling knives to people in their homes. The job entailed calling my parents, friends, and extended family, convincing them to allow me to come into their house, and pitching them to buy these knives. In reality, it was a commission-only job, but the company promised that if you didn't sell anything and make commissions, they would pay you $20 per appointment that you went and pitched, and each pitch was about an hour, hence the $20 per hour job.

As mentioned, I am an introvert, so I found the idea of randomly calling people and asking them to allow me to come into their houses and try to sell them knives intimidating. But my ambition for money, plus my lack of desire to take whatever crappy job my dad would have found me, outweighed my fears. I quickly found that I did not hate selling and that I actually liked it. More importantly, I realized that I was quite good at it. It felt natural to me. I looked at it like it was a game, which allowed me to get into the right mindset.

The first summer I did it, I had a one-hundred-percent close ratio, meaning the folks I pitched bought something for every appointment I went to. Now, it doesn't mean that everyone purchased an extensive set, but everyone bought something. Could some of this be out of pity that their friend's kid was putting themselves out there, or they didn't want to be perceived as a jerk by not buying something? Sure. Still, I was the only one in my office with that close ratio and was consistently on top of the sales leaderboard. By the end of the summer, I had made thousands of dollars, a fortune for a kid at the time, and I didn't have to work very hard to make it. Right then and there, my future was destined: I would be a salesperson. I was convinced. I was so sure that I even tried to convince my father that I didn't need to go to college and wanted to go straight into the workforce, but he wasn't having that. I am glad he didn't allow me to.

Everyone should have a sales job at some point in their life. There are so many life lessons you can learn from it. There are many lessons you learn and skills you develop through sales. Let's look at a few now. First off, you have to build communication skills. Sales teaches you quickly that you must learn to listen to what others are saying and communicate back in their language. If you don't, you will fail. Second, sales teaches you to be resilient. You have to be tough to succeed in sales, and you learn quickly people don't give a shit about you—they only give a shit about themselves. Next, sales teaches you to be empathetic. To sell anything to anyone, you must first put yourself in the shoes of the person you are selling to. Also, sales teach you negotiation skills that will last you a lifetime. In life, you get what you can negotiate. Finally, sales teach you about self-discipline. If you aren't disciplined and pick up the phone, guess what? You ain't making no money, Jack.

Do you think these skills correlate to being a successful entrepreneur or successful at anything in life? You bet your ass they do. This is the exact reason why whenever I get asked by younger people about what they should do post-college, if they are unsure of what they want to do, I tell them to get a job in sales. Even if they don't decide to pursue a career in it, the skills they learn will translate to whatever they do, and they will be stronger for it.

Now that we have discussed my undying love for sales and salespeople, let's discuss the fundamentals of when, who, and why you should bring salespeople into your organization.

TIMING OF WHEN TO BRING SALESPEOPLE AT THE BEGINNING OF THE COMPANY

For me, the first salesperson I hired, my good buddy Jeff Antone, came six months into the business. Jeff and I had worked together at EMC and were on the same sales team. He kept in touch with me during the first few months of Controle and told me he would love to join me at some point. I had to hold Jeff off because he would have come much sooner. But I could only ask people to join my company once I felt confident that A) the business would succeed and B) they were set up for success. I suggest the same to you. Salespeople are THE great catalyst to growing your company, but you must ensure they are set up for success. If you are starting the company solo or if you are the one doing the selling, the timing around them being set up for success should be obvious.

Six months into the business may or may not be the right timing for you; you can only determine that based on how things are going. My situation was unique; if it weren't for Jeff's persistence, I probably wouldn't have hired a salesperson until year two, as I was by nature more conservative in asking people to leave their livelihood to join my new venture. That changed as we matured, but you must do a gut check on what works for you. Now, let's discuss what to look for when hiring a salesperson.

WHAT TO LOOK FOR IN A SUCCESSFUL SALESPERSON

I have been in sales my entire career. During my travels, I have worked with and met thousands of salespeople. I know what bad looks like, what good looks like, and, most importantly, what great looks like. For salespeople, as with all winning cultures, you are looking for GREAT. Here are the key attributes you are looking for when hiring a great salesperson.

- **Good Listener**: Look out for the salesperson who never shuts up. When most people think of salespeople, they think of some extroverted person who is always talking. This is not the case for the most successful salespeople. You need someone who can listen as well as they can speak. As the saying goes, "You have two ears and one mouth for a reason."
- **Empathy:** To be successful in sales, you have to be able to see things from the other person's perspective. While this comes naturally to some, it can be a learned skill.
- **Competitive**: Pro tip: Look for people who played sports in their youth. They will typically have this competitive streak already built in. Additionally, a simple "How competitive are you?" question in interviews is a good one. If they immediately smile when you ask it, bingo.
- **Caring**: This one might come as a surprise, as most people think of salespeople as selfish. There are certainly those out there, but the best ones are unselfish; they want to help their customers, care about their success, and reap the rewards when they help them achieve it.
- **Customer-Focused:** You want salespeople who are MANIACAL about their customers' success and will do anything and everything to protect them. Ask them to give you examples of how they have been customer-focused. Jeff was a perfect example of this. He wanted to come and work with me

because he was sick of being asked to do what he felt was slimy or disrespectful to the customer. He wanted a job where he was rewarded for caring for the customer, not chastised because of it.
- **Coachable:** No matter how good they are, the best salespeople are always looking to improve and are coachable.
- **Persistent:** You have to be persistent in sales, and it would be one of the ten commandments.
- **Committed**: This is a hard one for many salespeople. I can't tell you how many people I have seen in sales jump from one job to the next, always looking for the next best thing. We used to call these people "lily pad hoppers," like frogs who jump from one lily pad to another. **AVOID lily pad hoppers at all costs**. You want people who will at least give you two years, and that is what I used to tell all the salespeople whom we interviewed. I used to say, "If you aren't willing to give us two years, don't take this job because you will be wasting mine and everyone else's time." In sales jobs, the first year is typically not going to go great as you build up your book of business. Usually, things won't be humming until year three. The good news is that you can quickly weed the lily pad hoppers out. Just look at their resume or LinkedIn profile. If they have never been at a place for more than two years, do not hire them, no matter what they say. Lily pad hoppers always have some story for why they are constantly moving around. Actions speak louder than words, Kermit.
- **Inquisitive**: Look for salespeople who ask a lot of questions. They will do the same to your customers, which is a good thing.
- **Tough**: Sales is a tough job. You are constantly living in the unknown and dealing with rejection. To be successful in sales, you have to develop tough skin. I knew this from experience, so I would try to figure out how tough people were during interviews. A good question to ask them to ascertain this is, "Tell me about a time in your life when you faced a significant obstacle and how you overcame it." Most people have heard this question and will immediately go to something about something that happened in their professional lives. But it's

more meaningful to hear something about their personal life. So, before they answer, I would always add, "And it does not have to be something you faced in your professional life. It can be, and preferably, something that has happened in your personal life." The stories that would come out of this question would be revealing and, many times, truly inspiring. It gives you a real sense of who they are and their makeup.

HOW TO STRUCTURE COMPENSATION AND COMMISSION PLANS IN THE BEGINNING

Show me the incentive, and I will show you the outcome.

CHARLIE MUNGER

In the beginning, one of the challenges you will face is how to best develop a compensation plan for salespeople. Most professional and experienced salespeople in Corporate America have a combination of a base salary and a commission plan on top. Consider bringing in experienced salespeople and, ideally, someone you already know. In the beginning, you will not have much time to hold their hands and develop them. You want to hire someone who believes in your mission but is experienced and self-sufficient. If you bring someone in with experience, you will likely have to devise a plan with some base salary.

I was fortunate. As mentioned, my buddy Jeff was coming to me asking to join me, and I had to keep pushing him back. He was relentless. So, I figured out a structure that would work for both of us. At the time, I still had no full-time W-2 employees. Six months in, I had about five employees, but all of them were 1099 contractors, and I only paid them when I needed them.

So, even though I still felt uncomfortable bringing on a salaried employee, I put myself in Jeff's shoes and made him an offer that I felt was fair to both of us. I offered him no base salary but a fifty percent commission, which is insane in the sales world. He would get half of every dollar of profit he brought into the company. Additionally, as I wanted to set him up for success, I knew that I would hand off several deals that I had been working on and that looked promising to him. I wanted him to get off to a fast start. Now, he was making roughly $125k in base salary and $125k in sales commissions opportunity at his current job and was the primary breadwinner for his family of five. So, this was still a significant risk for him.

Typical commission plans for companies like mine were around twenty percent commission up to thirty-five percent in accelerated commission after hitting your goals. So, for him to get fifty percent on day one was enticing, and he had enough confidence in himself and conviction in what I was doing. He had been hearing positive customer feedback, and I was open with him on how much money I was bringing in. So, he knew there was risk, but he also knew it was worth it with the potential upside. Jeff agreed to the deal without any hesitation. I remember him even saying, "Really?" as if he was surprised that I offered so much. But that is what you must do to get A+ talent; you must pay them and provide them with opportunities. Spoiler alert: Jeff made more in his first year (and far surpassed it in subsequent years) than at his previous job.

As mentioned, this was a bit of an anomaly. I wouldn't suggest you go out and ask people to take a sales job at no base and fifty percent commission, especially six months in when you are still unproven. That was just how it worked out for me. But once Jeff came in and crushed it right away, and we figured out what worked and what didn't, I felt confident that I could now formalize a program to bring in more salespeople.

A few months later, similarly to before, another of my ex-teammates at EMC contacted me proactively about joining our company. He was at a competitor, had lost a few deals to us, heard from Jeff how well he was doing and wanted in. However, he was in a much different position than Jeff and needed a base salary. I put him on a more traditional sales structure of a base salary and less of a percentage of the profits.

However, the key to the sales plan is this: incentivize them to what you want for the company. Many technology companies focus on driving gross revenue, but I was the opposite. I only cared about profitability since my company was bootstrapped, and I wanted to build a sustainable company. I tailored Jeff's and my first full-time salaried salesperson compensation to be focused solely on profitability. Salespeople are exceptional at maximizing their compensation plan, so ensure their compensation aligns with the company's goals, i.e., you want them to row the same way on the boat you are. Otherwise, you will go in circles.

BRINGING ON A SALES LEADER TO TAKE OFF

Like Jeff, my second salesperson had immediate success. As the novelist Paulo Coelho said, "If something happens once, don't expect it to ever happen again. But if something happens twice, it will almost certainly happen again." I felt this to be the case with the salespeople. At the time, I thought that Jeff's success might be an anomaly to him because of how amazing a salesperson he was and is. But for the second person, who had much less sales experience, to come in and crush it convinced me we had a winning platform.

By year three, we had four salespeople, all of whom had various degrees of success. I managed all of them, continued selling myself, and fulfilled all the other responsibilities of being the CEO of the company. It was becoming too much for me to handle. Although I loved working with the salespeople and strategizing on deals, it was also draining. I knew I needed all the strength to continue building the business. I knew it was time for me to bring on a sales leader. Choosing when to bring on a sales leader will depend on your specific situation, but the key markers are the following:

- Feeling like you are dropping the ball in other areas
- Feeling drained by working with the salespeople
- Feel like you cannot focus or do not have the time to bring more salespeople into the organization and proactively build the team

- Feel like the sales team and individuals are all doing their own thing with no defined processes

In my ongoing conversations with my mentor Dan, this was an area he pushed me on. He continually pushed me to give up responsibilities and, as he called it, "get things off my plate." In the first few years, my plate was always overflowing, and I was generally exhausted mentally at the end of every day. This is a common trap for entrepreneurs and especially control freaks like myself. When Dan questioned why I wasn't hiring more people to take on some of my responsibilities, I said, "Well, they won't do it as well as I will do it." He challenged me that, of course, they wouldn't do it as well as I was going to. The company was my baby, and I would always take more care of it than the babysitter. But that didn't matter; I had to give up my reins to grow. He pushed me hard to find a dedicated sales leader.

I listened and considered it. The conversation then changed from "Should I?" to "Whom it would be?" This is an area in which you will want to be proactive. Dan challenged me to think of the best sales managers or leaders I'd worked for and to write down all the attributes or actions they had that I admired or that worked well with me. I kept returning to my old manager at EMC, Dave, who I always felt was the best sales teacher I ever had and who got the most out of me. Additionally, I had many sales managers, but few were better at sales than me. That might sound arrogant, but that is how I felt. This manager was not only a great teacher, but after going on sales meetings with him, I was blown away by how good he was. And he was about the same age as me.

At that point in my career, I had only met ten or so salespeople in all my travels whom I considered to be better than me, and not only was Dave on the list of best managers I had, but he was also on this "better-than-me" list. I kept returning to all his attributes and how I could find them in someone else. Eventually, the thought popped into my head, "Shit, why look for a carbon copy of Dave? Maybe I should just go get Dave instead." The idea seemed preposterous. He made a lot of money at his job and had always been successful. He was the cream of the crop. Either way, I decided to reach out to him to grab lunch and catch up.

In that meeting, as if it were fate, he told me he was unhappy with the direction of his job and might start looking for a new one. I joked that he should join me. He seemed reluctant but didn't outright dismiss it. Months later, he joined us and was with us until the company's first sale years later. It was a great run and allowed me to focus on building the company, eventually priming us for sale and selling it. I couldn't have done that, or it would have made a near-impossible job even more challenging if I had not brought in a sales leader.

So, the point is this: When looking for a sales leader, look for someone you know already, with whom you can communicate well, and who is a proven commodity. Giving up the reins of sales was incredibly difficult for me, and even though Dave and I didn't always agree on everything, I trusted and respected him, and everything worked out in the end.

In conclusion, sales is the lifeline of the company's growth. But don't grasp at straws and grab just anyone. Salespeople will take up many of the company's resources, mental and otherwise. So, make sure these people are first aligned with your company's mission. Second, ensure their compensation plan aligns with the company's goals. Finally, when you have a proven model in place, as difficult as it may be for some, you must hand the reins off to someone who can be focused solely on building out the team so you can focus on the more strategic direction of the company. So now that we have figured this out, go sell something already, would you?

PHASE SEVEN
FINANCIAL INDEPENDENCE AND A LIFE WORTH LIVING

Well, folks, we have made it. This is the final phase of the journey. In this phase, we will explore the options and pros/cons of different exit strategies. We will discuss some hidden secrets on how to increase the value of your company by leaps and bounds, one that I wish I had known sooner. Finally, we will discuss why you NEED to be an entrepreneur, and if you sell or exit the company what lies on the other side. Are you ready? The finish line is in sight. Keep chugging.

CHAPTER 20
EXIT STRATEGIES AND WHAT TO KNOW WHEN BUILDING YOUR COMPANY

> *Selling a company isn't the end; it's a new beginning.*
>
> **WHITNEY WOLFE HERD, FOUNDER OF BUMBLE**

When I started my business, the thought of a potential exit, or in other words, the point where you leave the company via sale or some other vehicle, wasn't even on my radar. How would I possibly consider exiting the company when it had barely just begun? I didn't give it much thought. But as you grow and the business becomes more valuable, the thought will likely be forced upon you, either by friends and family asking if you have given it any thought or companies reaching out to you about your interest in selling. So, whether you like it or not, people will ask.

Even though you are most likely just at the beginning of starting your company, knowing some of the basics and benefits of exit strategies is crucial. As the saying goes, "All good things must come to an end." Looking back, I certainly wished I had known more about potentially selling the company and how to prepare for it so that I would be in a better position when I was ready. That is why I felt including this chapter in the book was necessary. I hope you'll take the lessons I've learned and build your company with the mindset that you'll sell it one day. I promise you and the company will be better off than if you gave it little thought as I did initially. By considering exit strategies early, you can be more proactive and less reactive when the time comes.

For the rest of the chapter, I will explain why you would want to potentially exit your company, the options available, and a critical game-changing lesson about increasing your company's value that I wish I had known sooner and will teach you. First, let's look at the pros and cons of selling or leaving the company, and I will share some of my experiences, having been through it and on the other side.

PROS OF HAVING AN EXIT STRATEGY

Many people view their business as their baby. It's a real emotional tie. So, the thought of leaving your baby or giving it to someone else is incredibly challenging for many. However, there are numerous compelling reasons to consider it. Let's explore them now:

1. **Profit Realization**: One of the primary advantages of having an exit strategy is the potential for significant financial gain. Not only can this be substantial, but it could be life-changing or potentially generations-of-your-family-life-changing financial gain. By selling your business, you can capitalize on the hard-earned equity you have built up. When you sell your business, your life will change, and most likely dramatically. It has been the event that opened the doors to all my dreams. Taking money for my hard-earned equity was the key to the door. I take a lot of shit for being retired so young. People routinely ask me, "How the hell did you retire at forty-five? I want to do the same." I always say, "It's simple: Start a company and sell it." It's not enough to start one; you also need to sell it.
2. **Risk Mitigation**: An exit strategy allows you to reduce personal risk. It provides a planned way to divest from the business before potential downturns affect wealth, market changes render the business less valuable, or some other problem or misstep makes the company difficult to continue.

This was something that used to keep me up at night. On paper, I was wealthy due to my stock in Controle. However, ninety percent of my net worth was in this stock. I had an uncomfortably disproportionate weight of my net worth invested in it. If something happened and the company couldn't survive, which certainly was realistic a handful of times, my net worth would evaporate. It wasn't until after I sold it the first time that I could take a deep breath from that perspective. Additionally, I have met a few entrepreneurs who had a chance to sell their companies but didn't for whatever reason. Most of the time, they didn't sell because they felt things would get better and wanted to maximize the value, only to have the market turn or some other unfortunate circumstance come up, causing the company to go out of business or lose the opportunity to sell. As you can imagine, they regretted not selling, and I could tell they kicked themselves about it every day. You can see it's harrowing for them. I heard several of these stories and told myself I didn't want to be like them. Good or bad, you can't predict the future, so if life-changing money is being dangled in front of your face, you listen.

3. **Opportunity for New Ventures**: Exiting one business provides the capital and time to pursue other projects or opportunities. This is particularly appealing for serial entrepreneurs or life-control freaks like myself. At some point, when I was running the business, I started to feel I had created my own self-imposed prison. I was sick of dealing with all the headaches and stress, and I wanted to be able to live my life more freely. By selling my company, I can pursue lifelong passions and dreams, including spending my days doing whatever I want to do and writing this book.

4. **Legacy Preservation**: Selling to a chosen successor or company that shares your vision can ensure that the business continues to operate in line with its founding principles. I had several offers from companies looking to buy us. The companies that had made these offers were all of different sizes and had various levels of perceived stability. Ultimately, I

chose the most stable and most prominent suitor as I felt it would be the greatest opportunity for growth and the safest option for preserving the company and my team once I stepped away. Due to the size and scope of the acquirer, I knew the company and my people would be in good hands going forward. And I was right. Here I am, over two years removed, while most of my team is still there and it continues to grow. It is hard to have the same level of confidence when running it solo or selling to a company with not as solid a track record as others.

5. **Reward for Effort**: An exit strategy can be the ultimate reward for the hard work and time you invested in growing the business. It provides a tangible measure of success and something you can hang your hat on for the rest of your life. It can be a reward for you, your employees, and loved ones who have supported you along the way.

CONS OF HAVING AN EXIT STRATEGY

For me, there haven't been many cons to selling the company. But I know I am unique, as I have heard some not-great things from others I have met. Let's look at the downside of an exit strategy.

1. **Loss of Control**: Once the company is sold, you lose control over its operations. This can be particularly difficult if the new owners take the company in a direction that differs from your vision. Fortunately, this wasn't a challenge for me, as the acquiring company and I were on the same page most of the time on how to grow it. But I have heard horror stories of entrepreneurs who were promised certain things would happen, only for the acquirer to go back on that promise and take the company in a different direction, resulting in a disaster for all parties.
2. **Emotional Impact**: For many entrepreneurs, their business is a labor of love, and letting go can be emotionally challenging. The identity and daily routine of running their business are often hard to replace. There have been several studies on how

it is common that when people sell their company, they feel depressed or lost. However, this was not the case for me, and I am glad I read some of the books discussing it before I sold so I could pay attention to my emotions. Many entrepreneurs wrap their identity in and around the business, so when they sell the company, they lose that identity and their sense of worth. Fortunately, for me, and I credit my meditation for much of this, my identity was never wrapped up in my title or the company. So, just because it happens to others doesn't mean it will happen to you.

3. **Potential Job Losses**: When a company is sold, especially to a larger firm, combining the two can mean duplications of roles and often lead to job cuts. This can affect your employee's morale and culture. However, I found there are ways to protect against this. I was loyal to my team and told all the potential acquirers that getting rid of any of them was off the table. Therefore, when I went under contract, I had the acquiring company ensure they wouldn't let go of anyone, and we walked through them all one by one to make sure there were no concerns. Ultimately, there was one role they felt they didn't need, but they told me they would find that person another job if he wanted it. Ultimately, he chose not to take it and left the company, but at least we got ahead of it. He had plenty of time to find a new job, and we parted amicably. Otherwise, they held their promise.

4. **Tax Implications**: The proceeds from the sale of a business can be substantial, leading to potentially significant tax liabilities, depending on the structure of the deal and the entrepreneur's personal tax situation. This is a bit complicated, but depending on the deal's structure, you could potentially have a large tax bill associated with a transaction without receiving immediate cash. Otherwise, if you sell the company and receive all the cash, expect the government to take twenty to thirty-five percent of your money, depending on your state. What a deal for them! They put no money into the company, did zero work, put up obstacles, took a large portion of your profits every year, and now get a big fat check

at the end. It's like having the worst business partner of all time! How do I get in on that racket? But, of course, you already know it's not like I am bitter about taxes or anything. Am I riiiiight?

5. **Dependency on Market Conditions**: The success of an exit strategy often depends on favorable market conditions. Economic downturns, poor timing, or industry declines can significantly reduce the value of the business at the time of sale. Yes, a lot of this will be out of your control. But that is why you hunker down during the down times and wait for the sun to shine again because it will. It is also the same reason that when the getting is good, don't be greedy and take the money off the table. Pigs get fat; hogs get slaughtered.

So, now that we have considered the pros and cons, let's examine the landscape of exit options. Each path contains its own set of considerations, benefits, and challenges.

OPTION 1: MERGERS AND ACQUISITIONS

Mergers and acquisitions (commonly referred to as M&A) are significant corporate finance transactions that involve consolidating companies or assets, typically aiming to enhance competitive advantage, expand reach, and achieve synergies. This is ultimately the route I took with my company, and a common phrase I heard during the courting phase about the potential synergies of the two companies was "one plus one equals three," meaning essentially, the two companies are stronger together than apart. I know the saying is cheesy, but you get the idea.

Though often used interchangeably, mergers and acquisitions have distinct meanings:

1. **Merger**: This occurs when two companies, usually of approximately similar size, agree to merge into a single new company rather than remain separately owned and operated.

This action is typically voluntary and seen as a merger of equals.
2. **Acquisition**: One company takes over another and establishes itself as the new owner. The target company does not change its legal name or structure but is owned by the acquiring company. This is what I did. I sold seventy percent of Controle to an organization called Epiq. Epiq became the majority owner of Controle, LLC. Controle operated as an independent company until I sold the remainder three and half years after the first purchase. Even though we were technically a separate company, we rebranded ourselves as Epiq and became a part of their team. Additionally, there were essentially no differences in outward appearances.

So, what are the objectives of M&A? Let's look at them now.

- **Growth**: Companies engage in M&A to accelerate growth by acquiring established operations and customer bases. When we were acquired, Epiq wanted to grow its business around Microsoft consulting and the other areas in which we competed against them. We wanted to tap into Epiq's sales teams, customer base, back operations, and global footprint to help meet our growth objectives.
- **Synergies:** These occur when the combined performance and financial results of a merged entity are greater than the sum of the parts due to increased efficiencies, reduced costs, or enhanced revenue opportunities— *à la* the old one plus one equals three. This did wind up playing out for us and Epiq. From a profitability perspective, we grew Epiq's department, which we competed with, 50x from when they acquired us, and for us, we grew over 500% in the three and a half years before I sold the remainder of my thirty percent of the business to them. And the company has continued to grow since I left. So yes, one plus one did equal three.
- **Increase Market Share**: A company can increase its market share by acquiring or merging with a competitor, often positioning it as a market leader. Epiq and Controle were two

of our space's top three Microsoft partners before we were acquired. After the acquisition, we were the clear leader and remain to this day.
- **Diversification**: Acquiring companies with different business lines or geographical locations reduces risk by diversifying business interests and stability.
- **Acquiring Talent and Technology**: This is especially common in technology sectors, where companies often acquire others to access specialized technology or talent. The story we discussed about Meta's acquisition of Oculus fits into this category.

While there are many benefits to M&A, there are challenges, and I witnessed them firsthand. Here they are:

- **Integration**: Merging two companies can be challenging due to cultural, system, and process differences. I went through this process, and trust me, it is not as easy as you would think. We didn't have Epiq email addresses until six months in, and it took us two years until we felt like we were truly integrated. Fortunately for us, the cultural differences, while not perfect, were pretty closely aligned, and we wound up making many friends at Epiq.
- **Costs**: The costs associated with M&A can be high, including legal fees, advisory fees, and integration costs. Further, you rack up many of these costs whether the deal goes through or not. I spent over $150,000 in fees before we were even acquired. If the deal didn't go through, I would have eaten all of that.
- **Regulatory Hurdles**: M&A can be subject to regulatory approval, and antitrust issues may arise, particularly with large, impactful transactions.
- **Risk of Failure**: Many mergers and acquisitions do not achieve their anticipated outcomes, often due to poor strategic fit, cultural clashes, or inadequate integration planning.

In summary, mergers and acquisitions are complex strategies companies use to strengthen their business, enter new markets, or gain new capabilities. While they offer significant opportunities for growth, they also come with risks that must be carefully managed to ensure successful integration and value creation.

OPTION 2: INITIAL PUBLIC OFFERING

Another exit route, and the dream of many entrepreneurs, is to take your company public through an initial public offering (IPO). I am sure many entrepreneurs have imagined ringing the bell on Wall Street on the day their company goes public. While seemingly glamorous, this path is less realistic for most companies. Statistically, it is estimated that less than one percent of companies ever complete an IPO due to the certain scale of operations and stringent listing requirements of exchanges. Either way, let's look at what this option looks like and the pros and cons.

An IPO is the process through which a private company issues shares of stock to the public for the first time. This involves selling shares to institutional and retail investors, broadening the shareholder base. Let's take, for example, our friends at Uber, whom we discussed earlier. On May 9, 2019, they were a private company, and you couldn't participate or invest in their future. On May 10, they went public, and now you could.

The following are the primary benefits of an IPO.

1. **Capital Raise**: One of the most significant benefits of an IPO is the ability to raise large amounts of cash. This infusion of funds is often used to invest in expansion projects, pay down debt, or fund other strategic initiatives that require significant capital outlay.
2. **Increased Public Profile**: Going public increases a company's visibility, credibility, and public profile, making it easier to attract new customers and business partners.

3. **Liquidity**: An IPO provides liquidity for shareholders and early investors, allowing them to sell their shares in the public market. This is particularly attractive for venture capitalists and founders who have invested in the company for years. Payday baby! IPOs have turned many entrepreneurs into billionaires overnight.
4. **Valuation**: Public companies often achieve higher valuations than their private counterparts due to increased transparency, regular scrutiny by market analysts, and a broadened investor base.
5. **Employee Incentives**: Public companies can offer more attractive compensation packages to their employees, including stock options and equity-based incentives. This can be a critical tool in attracting and retaining top talent.

While an IPO has many benefits, it also has challenges. Let's examine them now.

1. **Regulatory and Legal Requirements**: Going public requires compliance with extensive regulatory and legal standards, which can be costly and time-consuming. Additionally, companies must prepare for ongoing obligations like regular financial reporting and public disclosures.
2. **Market Pressure**: Public companies are under constant pressure from shareholders to meet quarterly earnings forecasts, which can lead to a focus on short-term performance at the expense of long-term strategy.
3. **Loss of Control**: Once public, a company's original owners and managers might find their control diluted. Shareholders and board members can exert significant influence, and the public and regulatory bodies often scrutinize actions. In some cases, not only can the founder lose control, but they can be ousted from the organization altogether against their will, as happened with Travis Kalanick of Uber.
4. **Cost**: The cost of an IPO can be substantial, including underwriting fees, legal costs, accounting expenses, and ongoing costs associated with being a public company.

In summary, an initial public offering can transform a company by providing a massive influx of financial capital, enhancing its corporate stature, and creating wealth opportunities for employees and investors. However, it also introduces new responsibilities and challenges that must be managed carefully.

OPTION 3: SUCCESSION PLANNING

Succession planning is a strategy for passing on leadership roles, and often the company's ownership, to an employee or group of employees, including family members. Also known as replacement planning, it ensures that businesses continue to run smoothly after the company's existing leaders move on to new opportunities, retire, or pass away. This is a common strategy for family-run or generational businesses. Have you ever seen the HBO TV show *Succession*? It is widely believed to be based on the real-world Murdoch family and their media empire.

Let's look at the pros of the succession planning approach:

- **Continuity**: Ensures continuity of operations and minimizes disruptions that can occur from a sudden departure of key individuals.
- **Preparedness**: Increases organizational readiness for unexpected leadership changes.
- **Employee Retention**: Motivates high-potential employees to stay in the organization with the promise of upward mobility.
- **Legacy Preservation**: Helps founders ensure that their vision and values continue to guide the company after they are no longer in charge.

There are also cons to succession planning. Just ask the Roy family. Let's look at them now:

- **Complexity**: Developing a robust succession plan can be complex and time-consuming. I mean how many seasons of Succession were there? Exactly.

- **Conflict**: Potential for conflict arises, especially in family-run businesses where multiple members may aspire to take over leadership roles. See all the Roy children here. Staring at you, Kendall.
- **Costs**: Associated costs with training and developing successors, as well as the potential for increased salaries and benefits to retain top talent.
- **Resistance to Change**: Existing leadership teams may resist passing on their responsibilities, especially if they are the founders, potentially leading to a clash between old and new visions for the company.

In conclusion, succession planning is a strategy for entrepreneurs to ensure a business's stability and longevity. It requires foresight, strategic planning, and commitment but offers substantial benefits by securing the company's future leadership. While the process can present challenges, including emotional, financial, and the Roy children all hating each other costs, in the real world, the advantages of a well-executed succession plan typically outweigh the drawbacks, making it an essential consideration for any entrepreneurial venture.

STRATEGIES TO THINK ABOUT WHILE RUNNING THE BUSINESS BUT WITH YOUR EXIT STRATEGY IN MIND

Now that we have looked at the options available, I will share some of my experience and discuss what I learned about increasing the value of my company that I wish I had known sooner when building it.

As mentioned before, in the early years, I gave little thought to my potential exit or sale of the company. Four years into the business, I had my first honest thoughts about it. We had made the Inc. 5000 list of the fastest-growing privately held companies. From our first year to the end of our fourth year, we had grown 403%, which made us the 994th fastest-growing privately held company in the United States, a fact I was incredibly proud of. It made it even more rewarding because I used to cold-call companies on this list, and now a company I created was on it. It was surreal.

When your company gets added to this list, you get a TON of calls and emails about buying or investing in the company. I was getting at least two dozen weekly calls and emails for months. It winds up being really annoying. After making the list, I talked to my buddy Justin Finnegan, whom we spoke about earlier in the book, about how annoyed I was getting all these calls. Justin's company had made the same list for years. He suggested that even though I had no interest in selling the company then, I should take some of these calls to gauge what these companies were looking for. If I did, I would be more prepared if or when I was ready to sell the company. This is precisely what he did, and he told me to look at it as if it was practice. I decided to take his advice.

This is where I took my first step into the fascinating world of M&A for Corporate America. Initially, I didn't do much due diligence on the companies with which I took the first few calls. I picked the first one I found in my inbox or the emails that, at least, I saw as being well-written. The first call I had was with a VC company, and it was brutal. I could tell I was dealing with a kid who was probably a few years out of college. He was cold calling to gather info and see if he could get a call set up for a more senior rep. But either way, since I had already blocked out the time, I just decided to stay on.

Immediately, this young whipper snapper went into a barrage of financial questions. "What is your annual revenue?" "What has been your annual revenue for the past three years?" "What was EBITDA (which stands for 'earnings before interest tax depreciation and amortization' and is an acronym for how much net profits you had) for the past twelve months?" "What has it been for every year for the past three years?" "What are projections for the next twelve months?"

It was a barrage of questions, all of which the answers to were sensitive information I didn't want to disclose to some stranger on the phone. Let's say it was somewhat of a quick call because I told him I would not share this information with just anyone, and then he huffed and puffed and hung up. *Ok, wow, that was a great start*, I thought to myself. But even from this brief interaction, I could tell that the companies calling me off this list could give two shits about what we solved for our customers or our strategy; they just wanted to know our hard-core financials. That was my first lesson. With M&A, it comes down to one thing and one thing only: the numbers.

Now that I was more prepared, I decided to look through the companies contacting me and try to find some that seemed reputable. There were some well-known VCs and private equity companies who had invested in companies in my space or well-known tech companies. Now that I had a good sense of what these calls would be like, I reached out to three of them and said that I would be interested in speaking, but I wanted to sign an NDA (nondisclosure agreement) so they wouldn't share the private information I would be providing. They had little incentive to share the information, but regardless, I am the son of an attorney and am always more careful in these scenarios.

The calls with these companies were much more beneficial. Of course, we did get into the financial aspects of the company. However, they also cared, or at least pretended to care, about hearing about the company's background, the market opportunity, and the go-forward plan. Each of the calls lasted about an hour. I was honest with them all in that I had no intention of selling or taking on investment (we didn't need money) but was open to discussion. Some of the calls were interesting, but they were all looking to either invest in the company or buy it. But where we were in the company's maturation, I wasn't ready for either option. Additionally, it felt like we were too immature to be acquired. Looking back at it, we were.

But the real benefit I got from these calls is that now I knew precisely what companies were looking for when investing or acquiring. One of the main lessons I learned was that it all seemed like a big game to me. And in this game, you would be in a good spot if you hit the markers they sought. They, pun intended, gave me the blueprint for selling a company. That left an impression on me and is something you should understand upfront.

Here are the primary markers:

- Gross revenue for the past three years and growth percentages
- EBITDA for the past three years and growth percentages
- Amount of recurring revenue (revenue that is contracted on a term that can be renewed going forward)
- Percent of project-based services
- Percent of services that were managed services-based
- Percent of revenue that was software sales (our proprietary IP)
- Year-over-year numbers for software sales
- Year-over-year numbers for recurring revenue
- 12-month projections
- 36-month projections

I noticed how they particularly keyed in on the amount of recurring revenue we had. At the time, this took me by a bit of surprise. I figured they would focus mainly on revenue and EBITDA numbers, but they didn't. I now know, but didn't then, that this became the holy grail of M&A: recurring revenue. Companies looking to invest in your company want as close to guaranteed future success. The way to do that is through recurring revenue or contracts with an annual fee that can be renewed. At the time, we had roughly ten to fifteen percent of our revenue as recurring, but these calls made me rethink that or at least explore why they cared so much.

So, I did what I usually do, the same process as in Chapter 1: I spoke to my entrepreneurial friends and read. I can't remember how I found it, but I read the book *Built to Sell* by John Warrillow. This is the book that I recommend when anyone asks to talk to me about selling their company and my experience. Even if you are not looking to sell, I recommend reading this book a few years into your journey. I wish I had done the same.

The book lays out in an easy-to-understand fashion the whys of selling your business and how best to structure it with the specific goal of selling it in mind. This is where my understanding and love of recurring revenue set in. The book says that the more guaranteed revenue you can have on an annual basis, the more valuable your company will become. If selling the business is all about the numbers (and it is), the driver of the multiple (how many times the market value is) comes down to the amount of recurring revenue you have. Let's look deeper into what recurring revenue is.

UNDERSTANDING RECURRING REVENUE

Recurring revenue is the financial backbone of many successful businesses, particularly those in the service and subscription sectors. Unlike one-time transactions, recurring revenue models provide ongoing income through regular customer payments. These payments are typically made monthly or annually in exchange for continued access to a product or service.

Types of Recurring Revenue Models

1. **Subscriptions**: These are common in software, media, and service industries, where customers pay a regular fee to access content or services. Examples include monthly subscriptions to business software or streaming services. Think of your Netflix subscription. The $29.95 fees to Netflix "reoccur" every month.
2. **Contracts**: Contracts are often used in telecommunications and business services, where clients enter into a contract agreeing to pay a fixed amount regularly for the duration of the contract. Think of your cell phone contract here. You agree to pay x amount of dollars per month and guarantee it on a three-year contract.
3. **Renewals**: These involve periodic renewals of licenses or services, such as yearly renewals of software licenses or maintenance contracts.
4. **Software as a Service (SaaS)**: This is a rapidly growing model over the past decade where businesses use cloud-based software on a subscription basis, paying ongoing fees to use the software rather than purchasing it outright. When you hear about applications that are "in the cloud," these are

typically just SaaS applications that you pay a monthly or annual fee to access. This is different from a decade ago when companies bought perpetual licenses for the software and owned it. Now, they don't have hefty upfront fees to purchase the software; they rent it annually. For example, my company's QuickBooks.com subscription was a SaaS offering.

Recurring revenue has many benefits, and they cannot be understated. Let's examine them now.

- **Predictability**: Recurring revenue provides a predictable stream of income that helps in budgeting and forecasting. It's a lot easier to predict future quarter revenues and think through increases in the budget when you have contracts already in place.
- **Stability**: Recurring revenue offers financial stability by ensuring revenue is not solely dependent on new sales. You will sleep much better at night knowing that you don't have to kill again tomorrow to eat. You already have some in the shed.
- **Customer Loyalty**: Recurring revenue encourages long-term customer relationships, as ongoing services or subscriptions deepen user engagement and loyalty.
- **Enhanced Valuation**: As mentioned, recurring revenue significantly increases your business's value, as investors and buyers value predictable and recurring income streams more. Just think to yourself, how much more would you pay for a company if it had close to guaranteed revenue versus one that didn't? Yep.

So, what did I do with this information now that I knew about the recurring revenue secret? I completely changed our company to a recurring revenue model. Even though, at the time, I wasn't completely sold on selling the company, I figured it wouldn't hurt to change this model in case we did, and regardless, the other benefits were clearly worth it on their own.

Tactics to Use to Switch to a Recurring Revenue Model

The first actionable step for me was to figure out how to change from our current model to a recurring revenue model. I decided one area in which we could make a change was for lower-end one-time service projects. In these scenarios, we would get introduced to a potential customer to help them either configure their new software solution or help troubleshoot their existing software. In these scenarios, it was unlikely that a customer wanted or would listen to a managed service right from the get-go. We usually had to prove ourselves first.

When we encountered these opportunities in the first four years of the business, we would give the customers what they wanted. If they wanted us to configure a new solution or troubleshoot, we would work with them to understand their requirements and then either provide them with a fixed-fee project cost or a time and materials hourly rate. Both of these models were transactional, meaning they were one-and-done.

In the mind of a company trying to buy or invest in your company, they could care less about these projects. How they looked at it was great for you, but why would we care, as that was in the past, with no guarantee that the customer would want to do anything in the future? Now that I understood the mind of the VC/PE firm, I decided that instead of providing the customer with a fixed fee or time and materials proposal, as we had been doing, we would now offer them an annual managed services proposal.

Let's look at what that would have looked like: Say the estimate we came up with internally is fifty hours to do the project. We had a $350 stock rate that we always used to determine cost. In that scenario, it would have cost the customer $17,500 for us to do the work. That dollar amount would not have excited us internally. We would take it, but really, we wanted six-figure projects. So, instead of going to the customer and saying the project cost would be $17,500, we told them we would give them a managed service cost for the same price of $17,500. The benefit to the customer is that they get to work with us on this initial project and receive months of our managed service support, essentially for free. For example, in Scenario A, we do the project, and it takes six to eight weeks or so to get it scheduled, do the work and test, and then say goodbye. And the customer has no additional support from us. But now, in Scenario B, they sign a twelve-month contract, we get the work done in the same eight weeks or so, and after we are done, they have ten months to work with us at no additional cost. This, my friends, is called the "no-brainer deal." I used to tell my reps to give customers deals so good that it was an absolute no-brainer.

A twelve-month managed service for a customer is much more valuable than a one-time project. Putting it at the same price makes it a no-brainer. The customer's immediate reaction becomes, "Ok, that sounds like a good deal, but how many years do I have to sign up for?" They ask this because most managed services or subscriptions are for three years. They think that is the catch. But we knew they would ask us this, and we got ahead of it. We told them the term is only for one year and that we are comfortable doing that because we feel confident that at the end of the year, they will see the value and want to re-up. We straight up told them that. Sometimes, we would still get some pushback, but roughly nine out of ten times, they would go for it. When they did, my team would become part of their team, and we would go above and beyond for them because getting them to renew was valuable to the organization. Our service became incredibly valuable to them, and now we didn't have to "sell" them on the value of the managed service. They already knew, and in the vast majority of these clients, they would renew in the second year.

So what was a potential one-time project-based customer that we probably would never speak to again now became a customer that could be an annual reoccurring contract, which made our business easier to run and predict, gave our sales people some almost guaranteed revenue and commissions going into the next year (which also, in turn, made it harder for them to leave us), and most importantly the client had a valuable member of their team to support whatever their challenges were and could focus on more prioritized work. And, of course, this recurring revenue made us much more valuable as a company. Win, win, win, win, win. No-brainer. My only regret about changing to this model is that I wish I had done it sooner.

By the time I was ready to sell the company, seventy percent of our revenue had been recurring, up from fifteen percent a few years prior. This made us an attractive company to buy and led us to receive a significant multiple on our valuation. So, the challenge and opportunity to ask yourself is how can you turn whatever you sell into a monthly or annual subscription. Just give it a shot and see how it goes. On top of all the massive benefits of running a business, it will make you much more valuable than if you don't. If I were to start another company, it would start as a recurring revenue company without even a second thought.

In conclusion, many view growing a business as giving birth to a baby and nurturing its growth. It is incredibly difficult for many to think about giving up on it or leaving it in the hands of someone else. However, a business is just that, a business. It's not a child. Considering an exit strategy is prudent and could be the best thing for you, your team, and your loved ones. You will know when the time is right, but know exiting the company is not an end, it's the door to a new beginning.

CHAPTER 21
YOU NEED TO BE AN ENTREPRENEUR— MASLOW'S HIERARCHY OF NEEDS

> *The story of the human race is the story of men and women selling themselves short.*
>
> ABRAHAM MASLOW

Well, friends, we are near the finish line and the end of our time together. We have learned a lot together, haven't we? Haven't we? Oh Lord, please say yes. For most of this book, we have talked about the nuts and bolts of starting and running a successful business. But before we leave each other, I want to go back to the beginning. Let's get back in touch about why you are doing this in the first place.

As complex as we may seem, human beings are quite simple. We all have the same basic needs. It's how we go about meeting them that separates us. The problem is that many of us get in our way. Most of us never meet our true potential because we focus on our short-term needs before giving any thought to our long-term goals. This short-term focus on needs versus goals shapes our behaviors and choices, often leading us to make decisions based on fear rather than opportunity. But you don't need to beat yourself up about it; it's our innate human nature. The best way to overcome this innate obstacle of focusing on short-term needs and getting in our way is to understand its roots.

In this chapter, we will discuss Maslow's hierarchy of human needs and why, after looking at them, it should be clear that you NEED to be an entrepreneur. As a background, Abraham Maslow is considered one of the founders of humanistic psychology. This perspective emphasizes individual potential and stresses the importance of growth and self-actualization. In 1943, in a paper entitled "A Theory of Human Motivation," he introduced Maslow's Hierarchy of Needs, a theory that proposed human beings are motivated and all of our actions are guided by a series of hierarchical needs, ranging from basic physiological to higher psychological and self-fulfillment ones. His life work has significantly influenced psychology, education, business, and several other fields.

Let's examine this hierarchy of needs and how entrepreneurship fits into this puzzle. It's a five-tier model depicted as hierarchical levels within a pyramid, as shown below.

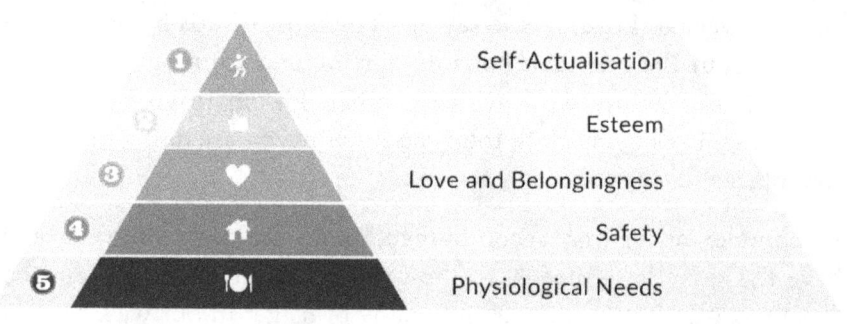

Ref:Temitope, F. (2023, June 29). *Maslow's hierarchy of needs: Understanding human motivation and well-being* (Digital image)

Let's look at the needs now, starting at the bottom.

PHYSIOLOGICAL NEEDS

These are the basic physical requirements for human survival, such as air, water, food, shelter, and sleep. According to Maslow, these needs must be satisfied before higher-level needs can be addressed.

Let's face it: Whether you like it or not, you need money to help with your physiological needs. You need money to put food on the table and provide shelter for your family. As we discussed, eighty-six percent of millionaires were self-made and created by starting a business. Who knows if you will become a millionaire? Being a millionaire doesn't matter; having stability and assurance to provide these fundamental needs does. Living in Corporate America, you walk in every day not knowing if you'll be fired, with the money faucet stopping in two weeks. Alternatively, you can start your own business, never have that risk, and have the potential reward of never worrying about having the resources to provide these needs ever again. Hmmm ... seems like an unbalanced risk-reward scenario to me. I know which one I am choosing. How about you?

SAFETY NEEDS

Once physiological needs are met, the second tier of needs relates to safety and security. This includes personal security, employment, resources, health, and property.

This need was number one for me. Because of the situation I dealt with when I was a teenager and the overwhelming feeling of being unsafe that followed, I made it my life mission to feel secure in all aspects of my life that I could personally control. As I have mentioned many times, I never, not ONCE, felt safe in any of my Corporate America jobs. I always felt like they could fire me at any moment, and it was a constant state of anxiety. The moment I fired my boss and stepped out on my own, I felt safer, and it wasn't even close. To this day, I have set up myself and my family for financial safety and security because of my entrepreneurial adventure. As an entrepreneur, you don't need to feel unsafe about employment because you are the employer. You can always fire yourself and find another opportunity, but you are one hundred percent in control of that decision.

Further, imagine how safe you will feel when you are a solo or the primary breadwinner for your family, have little kids, and suddenly, unexpectedly, you are out of a job. Do not fall into the common trap of thinking this won't happen to you because it does all the time. You are not untouchable. As of writing this sentence, this exact scenario has happened to five of my friends over the past six months. I can see the massive distress it has on them. They look genuinely terrified. Sadly, one of my friends even took his own life shortly after being let go from a job he had for over a decade. Only he knew what was going through his head and whether losing his job had anything to do with it, but he was the last person anyone expected to do it, which happened just weeks after he was let go. Do not underestimate this need to feel safe and in control and the reverse power of what happens when you take the reins.

LOVE AND BELONGING NEEDS

After physiological and safety needs are fulfilled, the third level of human needs is social and involves feelings of belongingness. This need for interpersonal relationships motivates behavior and involves friendships, romantic attachments, and family.

I have read many books and articles about how to develop happiness. A feeling of belonging to a community is always a critical component, and the one you hear is referenced the most in ascertaining one's level of happiness. We *homo sapiens* are pack animals, and we need our pack to feel complete. Entrepreneurship creates community. If you have ever been on a sports team, you know what it feels like to work with others toward a common goal, and this is one of the reasons, especially in our youth, that we make such great friends through sports. Business is the ultimate adult sport. When running a company, you and your team work toward common goals, and when you achieve them, share in the rewards. This sense of accomplishment and doing it together creates an intense bond and an incredible feeling of community.

Further, the broader entrepreneurship community you enter will build another community you belong to. Whenever I see any of my entrepreneur friends, I get giddy. It is hard to describe, but we have a deep connection to each other, even if we never worked together. We can discuss things with each other that no one else will understand. We know what it takes to do what the other did, and it creates genuine respect and admiration for each other. Additionally, this is true for those entrepreneurs I just meet—you get each other right away, and an immediate bond is created. You are part of this secret group that no one else can understand and few enter.

Further, for all of the entrepreneurs I have been quoting in this book, I don't know any of them personally, but I understand them and feel a real kinship toward them as if I do. So yes, if needing a community is a fundamental need for us humans, you will get it by being an entrepreneur.

ESTEEM NEEDS

The fourth layer includes needs related to self-esteem, respect from others, and recognition. These needs relate to the desire to be accepted and valued by others.

Boy, oh boy, entrepreneurship is a no-brainer path for those seeking self-esteem and respect. First and foremost, and most importantly, you will have self-respect. As Dan mentioned in one of my early meetings, he told me that the moment I go out on my own I would respect myself more for the mere fact that I dared to do it. He was right. Since getting through my PTSD, I never really had a problem with self-esteem or confidence, but wowsers, it increased by putting myself out there, staring fear in its face, and pushing through the finish line. My self-esteem is so strong now that I do everything I can to deflect praise, push it back on the person giving it to me or others, or, in general, try to be self-deprecating. Quite simply, my bucket is already full. Entrepreneurship was a big part of that.

If stroking your ego or gaining respect from others fills your bucket, you will get it in spades as an entrepreneur. Once you succeed in business, others around you will boost your self-esteem. People will develop a more inflated opinion of you than you probably have of yourself. It's almost like a rock star status. Especially in larger business environments like conferences, you will feel people pointing at you and knowing who you are before you even meet them. It takes a minute to adjust to. Further, being a CEO, people will kiss your ass just because they think they can get something from you. You have to be careful because your ego can destroy all things good, but regardless, you will receive heavy praise and respect. I have thought about why you get so much, and I believe it comes down to the fact that almost everyone has thought about starting their own business, but fear has stopped them. They admire those who pushed through what they couldn't.

If you succeed, you will also have it in spades. The recognition we received for being on the Inc. 5000 was astonishing. We had also won many awards from our partners and made many other fast-growing lists. We had to buy a whole shelf to display the trophies in our office. Business is the ultimate adult sport; if recognition is the trophy you want, be prepared to have a dedicated space in your office for it.

SELF-ACTUALIZATION NEEDS

At the top of the hierarchy, self-actualization refers to a person's full potential and its realization. Maslow describes this as the desire to accomplish everything that one can and become the most that one can be.

Entrepreneurship will push you to be the best person you can become, whether you like it or not. You will be pushed way out of your comfort zone and find out what happens when you do. There is always something new to learn. You will develop skills in areas you never even considered (OHHH SNAPS! Kevvie can call out the accountant's bullshit, y'all!). You will be forced into uncomfortable situations. You will be forced to make difficult decisions. You will be presented with opportunities you never dreamed of and discover what happens when you do. You will be forced to reach deep and discover what you are truly made of. When you face all these challenges and opportunities and come out on the other side, a beautiful thing happens: You find out what you are TRULY made of. For me, I always felt like I could be successful in running a company. I didn't care about proving it to anyone else; I wanted to prove it to myself. And I did. As a result, I now have a level of calm and peace I can't even find the words to describe. For the rest of my life, I KNOW what I am capable of. When I am sitting on my death bed, I won't be thinking, "What if?" I know. That is a gift I wish for everyone.

So, what of these needs most strike you? Are you anxious about providing for yourself and your family and looking for a better path than the one you are on now? Do you crave safety, security, and control of your life like I did? Do you want to have a higher sense of belonging to a community? Do you want to be the admiration of others and, more importantly, to yourself? Do you want to know what you truly can become? Do you want to not always wonder to yourself *what if?* If you said yes to any of these, entrepreneurship is the safest and most direct path. Don't believe me? Fine. I challenge you to go back through your fundamental needs and argue how having a nine-to-five employee job would better meet them and be the more effective approach. Go ahead, do it right now.

I'm still waiting. Couldn't do it, could you? Bet.

CHAPTER 22
THE LONG-TERM GAIN

> *Entrepreneurs live a few years of their life like no one else will, so they can live the rest of their life like no one else can.*
>
> *ANONYMOUS*

Imagine waking up every day and doing exactly what you wanted to do. No boss is demanding anything of you. You don't have to do that task at work, which you know wastes your precious time (TPS reports, anyone?). You can wake up when you want. You don't feel rushed to do anything. You can choose to do what you want when you want and with whom you want. You don't wake up daily worrying about how you will pay your bills or save for the future. What would you pay for that level of freedom? What would you do with this newfound time?

Well, I am here to tell you that this scenario exists and is very real. This level of freedom is the pot of gold at the end of the rainbow for the entrepreneur. Sure, entrepreneurship's financial and self-fulfillment rewards can be amazing, but for me, the real goal was freedom. At forty-five years old, I achieved this freedom. And unless you are from a wealthy family (I certainly wasn't), the likelihood of waking up at forty-five and doing whatever the hell you want to do is doubtful without the path of entrepreneurship.

I know I sound like a broken record, but it's not that complicated. If you want wealth, freedom, recognition, or whatever the hell you are looking for, entrepreneurship is THE path. Now, is it an easy path? No, it's not. I am not going to sugarcoat it. As discussed throughout this book, it is not easy; if it were, everyone would do it. But I am here to tell you not to worry about easy, worry about possible. Is it possible to live the rest of your life in ways you could only dream of? Yes, it is. Trust me, if I can do it—and you have seen what a moron I am—you can too. We discussed the parts that make starting and running a successful business hard. We have answers for them and discuss how to tackle them throughout this book. So, no more excuses. In your hands, you now have THE BLUEPRINT. So, what will you do with it?

Let's be honest. Life is too short, way too short. We are all living on borrowed time. *Tick, tock, tick, tock.* Would you rather spend your limited time supporting someone else's dream or working on your own? You owe it to yourself and your loved ones to discover what you are made of. I am here to tell you that you are more than capable. I KNOW you can do this.

Don't believe me that entrepreneurship is still THE PATH? Fine, jerk-face, don't take it from me; let's hear from some other entrepreneurs:

- "Your time is limited, so don't waste it living someone else's life. Don't be trapped by dogma—which is living with the results of other people's thinking." – Steve Jobs
- "Twenty years from now, you will be more disappointed by the things that you didn't do than by the ones you did do." – Mark Twain
- "One day, you will wake up, and there won't be any more time to do the things you've always wanted. Do it now," – Paulo Cohelo
- "Life is either a daring adventure or nothing at all." – Helen Keller
- "The most difficult thing is the decision to act, the rest is merely tenacity." – Amelia Earhart

Let's also hear from some of the other entrepreneurs we met throughout the book (in order of appearance)

Marc Lifshin: "If you ever collected sports cards (or still do, like me) you know rookie cards are the most sought after. They give us the first glimpse at a player's genius and tell the first chapter in a story that changed the game. When I look at my favorite rookie cards now, they remind me of the mindset you need to start your own company. It takes holding onto that rookie edge your entire career—always training, growing, and competing. Staying tenacious and inspired and absolutely outworking everyone.

Many people think starting a business means living the dream—no boss, flexible schedule, and quick success. Many people think starting a business is completely irrational because the odds of success are so low. They're both right. Starting your own business means giving up your work-life balance and throwing all your chips back into the company. But if you believe in it and are passionate about it, you'll love every minute, and it will be one of the most rewarding decisions you'll ever make.

So, if you're thinking of starting your own company, I have two pieces of advice. First, surround yourself with naysayers because they'll put the chip on your shoulder that helps you keep a rookie mindset and go crush. Second, stop waiting for the perfect time to do it because it will never come. Just believe in yourself and go all in.

Now go start something that changes your life, and maybe even the world."

Dan "The Man" Adamany: "Entrepreneurship is a path everyone talks about, but very few people take. The path is most traveled by the young or the optionless. It is most difficult to make the decision when you are having success in your career. Your opportunity cost is much higher, hence the risk seems much greater. In order to take the path, you need to believe in yourself and believe you can do something better than anyone else. As Kevin noted, money, praise, respect, and all these things people give to successful entrepreneurs are not the best gifts. The best gift is pride. Being proud that you took a risk that so many others wouldn't. Proud that you were successful despite others telling you that you wouldn't. Proud that you took the path so many others just think about taking.

Saying all of this, there is always another mountain to climb. I have learned this year after year as my company has grown. The same things that drive you to start a business are the same things that push you to grow your business. When is it enough? When do you change gears? What more can I learn? How much bigger can we get? Personally, I am still searching for those answers. One of the most rewarding things for me now is helping others, like Kevin. This applies to helping entrepreneurs or it could be people within AHEAD. Nothing is more satisfying than playing a role in someone else's success. When it is all said and done, that is the legacy and the impact that lives on."

Justin Finnegan: "My journey towards entrepreneurship began on a very cold February day in Minnesota in 2000. I was a young consultant with a big firm. This was the height of the first dot.com boom, and one of our clients had the idea to spin off a solution they had developed into a software company. My assignment was to help them set up an organization to implement the solution. I put together a plan for a consulting organization and they told me great, we need you to start interviewing candidates to work on that team. The solution was based on a legacy system, and there was a lot of available talent, so I set up a bunch of interviews and got to it.

It became apparent that almost all of the people I interviewed had worked for exactly one company in their careers, in all cases, for over 20 years. They had all been laid off, replaced with younger/cheaper labor, or their jobs had been sent offshore. I was, in most cases, twenty or thirty years younger than the candidates, and it got to the point that I could tell without looking at their resumes how long they had been out of work. The ones who were recent and were still receiving severance couldn't believe they were talking to me and would ask questions like, 'When will I talk to an actual manager?'. The ones who had been out for over a year were practically begging; it was clear that this was the first interview they had in months. It was apparent to me that almost none of these people would ever get another job anywhere near the salary they had before, but more importantly, with anywhere near the status and security.

That day planted the seed that I never wanted to be one of those people. They had worked hard, played the game, put in their time….and were stuck. I couldn't imagine that being me. I knew that meant I would have to take risks, constantly evolve and, most importantly, take control of my own success.

I think that's the core driver for entrepreneurs: the need to be at the helm of your own ship and the confidence to do so. Deciding that (what looks like) the safe path isn't for you is the first step.

That day led me on a 20-year journey to build practices and companies, which I am still doing today. I've had the opportunity to help people build great careers and have developed lifelong friendships. I wouldn't change a thing."

Amen. Thinking through all their advice, my advice to you would be to heed these brilliant Entrepreneur's advice. All three of them have taken control of their life, and I can tell you, knowing them all personally, they all have a level of self-pride and confidence not commonly found in others. There is a clear reason for that.

THE LONG-TERM GAIN

As we discussed earlier in the book, in the early years of the business, I repeated a mantra to my wife and, frankly, to myself to remind us why we were making all these sacrifices. It was "Short-term sacrifice for a long-term gain." So, what does the long-term gain look like? The beautiful answer is whatever you want. You become the artist, and your life becomes your canvas.

I live a surreal life now. I have been retired for over two years, but I often question whether it is even real. It's emotional for me to think about where I started and where I am now. I do get a lot of grief from my family and friends about it. Want to know the number one question I get? It's "What the hell do you do every day?" For a while, I felt guilty about responding to this question and would attempt to break down what I did. At one point, I just got sick of answering and, out of frustration, one day answered, "Whatever the hell I want to do." And that is the point. I feel like Andy Dufrane in *Shawshank Redemption*. I feel like I crawled through a river of shit to come out on the other side. And the other side is indeed beautiful. Zihuatanejo.

As you know, my WHY was that I wanted to control my future and spend the rest of my days doing what I wanted to do, not what others wanted me to do. So what does that look like? As of this writing, my children still live under my roof. I have a seventeen-year-old daughter, a fourteen-year-old son, and a nine-year-old son. It is important for me to be physically and mentally present during these years, especially because I feel I missed out on a lot when I was running the company. Recently, I read an article that discussed how our children are only in our lives on a day-to-day basis for a short period. In it, they say that by the time your kids are eighteen, ninety percent of your time together will have already been spent.

I was gone for many years and now want to be around them as much as possible. I coach everything, drop them off and pick them up from school, spend time with them at night and on the weekends (when they want to, at least), and get the opportunity to do a lot of Daddy Daughter or Daddy Dude dates. This time is so precious to me. The time I have to spend with them is the biggest gift I could ever give them, and in return, be given to me. This is all due to my entrepreneurial adventure.

Additionally, for the years I was running the company, my wife Jeannette and I had little time to ourselves, and when we did, I was distracted. I would be lying if I didn't admit that our marriage was rocky at times. But through it all, we persevered, and our relationship is stronger now than ever. We now have the time and energy to work on our relationship. And it has worked. We do many things together and have a lot of fun. Additionally, I am an active participant in the day-to-day activities with the kids, which has freed her up to follow her dreams, including starting her own interior design business, which has been a huge success for her. It's her time now, and I feel so grateful to help her chase her dreams as she supported me in chasing mine.

Jeannette Barnicle: "Starting your own business can be the most intimidating process of your life. Running your business can bring some of the most perplexing and frustrating challenges. However, overcoming these fears and obstacles can lead you to the most fulfilling moments in your professional life while giving you rare opportunities in your private life. I couldn't be prouder of the entrepreneurs in my life, especially my husband. I have been fortunate enough to be a part of and benefit from Controle and Kevin's hard work. He has put our family in a position I do not believe would be possible otherwise."

Now that you have this newfound time to spend with family and friends, you can also chase down any other crazier lifelong dreams. For me, there were a few dreams I always had as a kid. First, I always dreamed of writing and directing a comedy movie. I LOVE comedies. As a kid, my little brother and I would constantly watch comedies. Some of my all-time favorites are *Spaceballs*, *Trading Places*, *Blazing Saddles*, *Caddyshack*, *The Vacation* movies, and *Old School*. We would constantly, and still do, comment on everyday life scenarios and conversations with lines from these movies. It was like this secret little language we had. It drove my mom crazy. She used to say, "If you idiots spent as much time on school as you do quoting movies, you would be going to Harvard." Quite simply, I love to laugh. I feel like it's one of the most important attributes I can pass on to my kids: the love of laughter. Because, let's face it, life can be hard, and if you don't laugh at the absurdity of it all, you can wind up losing your mind. The world is a crazy place these days, and I wish there were more laughter.

So, with my newfound time, I decided to chase this crazy dream and produce a comedy. Ok, so I have absolutely no fucking clue what I am doing and have zero prior experience, but I am still going for it. I am still working on it, but you can see the trailer here: https://bit.ly/PaddleMovie. The movie is about this crazy sport I picked up as an adult called Platform Tennis, or Paddle for short, that I love, and I find absolutely hilarious how serious all these working adults, me included, take it. Men and women all over the country are on Paddle teams and play other teams, and we all act like absolute lunatics about it. I thought it would be funny to document a season and show the absurdity of it all. Will anything come out of the movie? Who knows. I have no clue. And you know what? It doesn't matter. My entrepreneurial adventure has allowed me to go for it, and I have zero financial or time pressure associated with it. Also, because there is no pressure, I can swing for the fences, just like I am doing with this book. That is a long-term gain.

Otherwise, guess what I always thought my profession would be as a kid? Besides dreaming of being an NBA player (unfortunately, that dream died when I was born), I wanted to be a writer. As a kid, I would write short stories. In college, I wrote a book about the shooting I went through and the impact it had on me. I never meant for it to be published; I just gave it to my closest friends and family so they could know why I had changed so much but also that I was ok. I also wrote poetry in college, which I found therapeutic in dealing with the emotions associated with my PTSD, and I was published in several books. I enjoy the process of writing. I feel like something is compelling and timeless about the written word. Books contain the secrets to life. So, what am I doing now that I have free time? Yep, you guessed it and are consuming it now. I am writing. And I hope it can become my "career" for this next phase of my life. My goals with writing are simple: I feel very grateful for all I have been given, and I want to give back.

Now, maybe you will love this book (and if you please, please, please give me a review online, mmm'kay?), or perhaps you will hate it (seriously? I thought we were friends!). Maybe it will be successful, and maybe it won't. It doesn't matter. I enjoyed doing it and have no financial or time pressure tied to it. Also, one day, I hope my kids will read it; it will inspire them, and if nothing else, maybe they can use it to better understand their goofball dad. Long-term gain.

So, ask yourself, what do you want to do when you achieve financial and time independence? Write it down and use it as motivation. I am here to tell you that it is absolutely achievable. Find your long-term gain and go after it.

Before we go, I want to thank you. Thank you for getting this far and sharing your precious time with me. It is not something I take lightly. I really tried to make this book as valuable to you as possible. Writing this book has been therapeutic (fuck you, taxman!) and nostalgic for me. Writing for you has allowed me to reflect on my entrepreneurial journey, with its highs and lows, twists and turns, and life-changing experiences. I'm reminded of why I embarked on this adventure in the first place. It has shaped my life in ways I could have never imagined, teaching me about business, yes, but also about resilience, passion, and the power of believing in oneself. It's a journey I'd sign up for all over again, and I'm so excited for you to carve your path.

Before we part, know this does not need to be goodbye. Don't be shy about contacting me at Kevvie@itstheblueprint.com with any questions. Further, I would love to hear about your success! I hope we can build a Blueprint Squad community and support each other along the way.

Finally, remember that entrepreneurship is all about the journey. Enjoy every step, learn from every stumble, keep moving forward, and give 'em hell. Here's to your dreams, to your success, and to the incredible adventure that awaits you. You got this shit.

Cheers,

Kevin Barnicle

#blueprintsquad

REFERENCE LIST

Addair, G. (n.d.). Everything you've ever wanted is on the other side of fear [Quote]. Good News Network. https://www.goodnewsnetwork.org

Apple Inc. (1997). Think different [Television commercial]. TBWA\Chiat\Day. https://fs.blog/steve-jobs-crazy-ones/

Armstrong, J. (Creator). (2018–2023). *Succession* [TV series]. HBO

Bezos, J. (n.d.). The most important single thing is to focus obsessively on the customer. SucceedFeed. Retrieved from https://succeedfeed.com/jeff-bezos-quotes-about-business/

Bezos, J. (2016, August 23). Your brand is what people say about you when you're not in the room. HuffPost. https://www.huffpost.com/

Blakely, S. (2020). About SPANX: The founding story. Spanx. https://www.spanx.com

Blakely, S. (2020). How she built a billion-dollar business from scratch. Fox Business. Retrieved from https://www.foxbusiness.com

Branson, R. (n.d.). Business opportunities are like buses, there's always another one coming [Quote]. BrainyQuote. https://www.brainyquote.com/quotes/richard_branson_183468

Buffett, W. (2015, October 10). 15 quotes from Warren Buffett that take you inside the mind of a legendary investor. Business Insider. https://www.businessinsider.com

Carrey, J. (Performer). (1994). To train zee dolphin, you must zink like zee dolphin! You must be getting inside zee dolphin's head [Quote]. In T. Shadyac (Director), *Ace Ventura: Pet Detective* [Film]. Warner Bros

Churchill, W. S. (2013). *Winston Churchill: The greatest quotations*. Bloomsbury

Chouinard, Y. (2010). Patagonia's reluctant businessman. Blue Ridge Outdoors. Retrieved from https://www.blueridgeoutdoors.com

Cialdini, R. B. (2006). *Influence: The psychology of persuasion* (Revised ed.). Harper Business

Coelho, P. (n.d.). Quote. Retrieved from https://www.goodreads.com/quotes/123456

Churchill, W. S. (2013). *Winston Churchill: The greatest quotations*. Bloomsbury

Darabont, F. (Director). (1994). *The Shawshank Redemption* [Motion picture]. Columbia Pictures

Drucker, P. F. (1989). Public Papers of the Presidents of the United States: Ronald Reagan, p. 1140. Also quoted in *The Wit and Wisdom of Wall Street* (Dow Jones-Irwin, 1985), p. 26

Earhart, A. (1932). *The fun of it*. Harcourt, Brace and Company

Engadget. (2014, March 26). Oculus Rift: From $2.4 million Kickstarter to $2 billion sale. Engadget. Retrieved from https://www.engadget.com

Ferriss, T. (2009). *The 4-hour workweek: Escape 9-5, live anywhere, and join the new rich* (Expanded and updated ed.). Harmony Books

Ferriss, T. (2009). *The 4-hour workweek: Escape 9-5, live anywhere, and join the new rich* (Expanded and updated ed.). Crown Publishing Group

Ferriss, T. (2010). *The 4-hour body: An uncommon guide to rapid fat-loss, incredible sex, and becoming superhuman.* Crown Archetype

Ferriss, T. (Host). (2015, September 25). The scariest Navy SEAL I've ever met... and what he taught me [Audio podcast episode]. In *The Tim Ferriss Show*. Tim Ferriss. https://timferriss.libsyn.com/the-scariest-navy-seal-ive-ever-metand-what-he-taught-me

Ferriss, T. (n.d.). My favorite "smart drugs". Tim Ferriss Blog. https://tim.blog/2016/09/21/my-favorite-smart-drugs/

Gillett, R. (2015, May 18). From welfare to one of the world's wealthiest women — the incredible rags-to-riches story of J.K. Rowling. Business Insider. https://www.businessinsider.com/the-rags-to-riches-story-of-jk-rowling-2015-5

Google. (n.d.). How we started and where we are today. Google. https://about.google/intl/en_id/our-story/

Hoffman, R. (n.d.). The fastest way to change yourself is to hang out with people who are already the way you want to be [Quote]. AZ Quotes. https://www.azquotes.com/quote/520979

Hoffman, R. (n.d.). Starting your own business isn't just a job—it's a way of life. Elevate Society. https://elevatesociety.com/starting-your-own-business-isnt/

Horowitz, B. (2014). *The hard thing about hard things: Building a business when there are no easy answers.* Harper Business

Huffington, A. (2016). *The Sleep Revolution: Transforming Your Life, One Night at a Time.* Harmony.

Jobs, S. (1997, June). *Apple Worldwide Developers Conference.* Apple. Retrieved from https://www.apple.com

Kalanick, T. (2010, December 22). Uber's founding. Uber Newsroom. https://www.uber.com

Keller, H. (1957). *The open door.* International Publishers

Kim, W. C., & Mauborgne, R. (2005). *Blue ocean strategy: How to create uncontested market space and make the competition irrelevant.* Harvard Business Review Press

Musk, E. (n.d.). The complete list of companies owned by Elon Musk. Fabrik Brands. https://fabrikbrands.com

McCartney, P. (n.d.). Transcendental meditation gives me an island of calm in the midst of so much turbulence [Quote]. AZ Quotes. https://www.azquotes.com/quote/890168

Michalowicz, M. (2008). *The toilet paper entrepreneur: The tell-it-like-it-is guide to cleaning up in business, even if you are at the end of your roll.* Obsidian Press

Moore, G. A. (1991). *Crossing the chasm: Marketing and selling high-tech products to mainstream customers.* HarperBusiness

Munger, C. T. (2005). *Poor Charlie's Almanack: The Wit and Wisdom of Charles T. Munger* (P. D. Kaufman, Ed.). Donning Company Publisher

Mycoskie, B. (2014). TOMS CEO expanding reach of 'Buy One Give One' model. Fox Business. https://www.foxbusiness.com

National Small Business Association. (2023). *Economic report on small businesses.* NSBA. https://www.nsba.biz

Rand, A. (1943). *The Fountainhead.* Bobbs-Merrill.

Ries, E. (2011). *The lean startup: How today's entrepreneurs use continuous innovation to create radically successful businesses.* Crown Business

Sequoia Capital. (2014). WhatsApp milestone: Four numbers that explain why Facebook acquired WhatsApp. Sequoia Capital. Retrieved from https://www.sequoiacap.com

Seuss, D. (1990). *Oh, the places you'll go!.* Random House

Systrom, K. (2015, February 19). How a humble stray dog helped launch Instagram. Marketplace. https://www.marketplace.org/2015/02/19/how-humble-stray-dog-helped-launch-instagram/

Temitope, F. (2023, June 29). *Maslow's hierarchy of needs: Understanding human motivation and well-being* [Digital image]. Medium. https://medium.com/@temitopefocus12/maslows-hierarchy-of-needs-understanding-human-motivation-and-well-being-9269b5e9b52d

The Coca-Cola Company. (2011, March 1). Honest Tea joins the Coca-Cola family. The Coca-Cola Company. Retrieved from https://investors.coca-colacompany.com

Twain, M. (1935). *Mark Twain's notebook* (A. B. Paine, Ed.). Harper & Brothers

Urban, T. (2015, December 8). The tail end. Wait But Why. https://waitbutwhy.com/2015/12/the-tail-end.html

Wikipedia. (n.d.). Pebble (watch). Wikipedia. Retrieved from https://en.wikipedia.org/wiki/Pebble_(watch)

Willink, J. (2015). *Discipline equals freedom: Field manual.* Jocko Publishing

Wolfe Herd, W. (n.d.). Selling a company isn't the end; it's a new beginning [Quote]. Next Biography. https://www.nextbiography.com

Wu-Tang Clan. (1993). C.R.E.A.M. On *Enter the Wu-Tang (36 Chambers)* [Song]. Loud Records

Zuckerberg, M. (n.d.). The biggest risk is not taking any risk. BrainyQuote. https://www.brainyquote.com/quotes/mark_zuckerberg_453450

APPENDIX

Hey you, where you going?! Don't you want more information and goodies??? Of course you do, you animal! And good news, you are in luck girlfriend! Just remember to give The Blueprint an honest review (I need the social proof bruh!) and email me either a screenshot or link to the review to review@itstheblueprint.com and you will get the following bonuses!

- Controle's business plan
- List of startup and ongoing business expenses
- Additional information on how to use your 401k to fund your business using ROBS (Rollovers as Business Startups)
- Branding: what different colors mean
- Branding: what different typographies mean

But, wait, THERE'S MORE! (Do I sound like an infomercial? GOOD!) You will also receive (just because I love you):

- Kevvie's recommended business books to read (I have read most of them and curated the best just for you)
- Kevvie's Top 10 sleep hacks
- Dr Sue amazing life coach/Therapist contact info
- The Blueprint Squad 10% off friends and family discount code to use at any of my vacation rental properties
- And maybe more! (I may feel frisky as time goes on)

www.ingramcontent.com/pod-product-compliance
Lightning Source LLC
Chambersburg PA
CBHW020804171224
R15991000002B/R159910PG18974CBX00002B/1